UNIVERSITY OF NORTH CAROLINA
STUDIES IN THE ROMANCE LANGUAGES AND LITERATURES
Number 68

TRAGIC THEORY AND
THE EIGHTEENTH-CENTURY FRENCH CRITICS

TRAGIC THEORY AND
THE EIGHTEENTH-CENTURY FRENCH CRITICS

BY

JAMES HERBERT DAVIS, JR.

CHAPEL HILL

THE UNIVERSITY OF NORTH CAROLINA PRESS

DEPÓSITO LEGAL: V. 3.237 - 1966

ARTES GRÁFICAS SOLER, S. A. - JÁVEA, 30 - VALENCIA (8) - 1967

PREFACE

With the passing of Racine, French tragedy enters a period of decline. The playwrights of the new age, desiring to imitate the dramatic creations of the seventeenth century, and seeking vainly to attain the artistry of their predecessors, find themselves hampered by a fear of the *naturel,* by the demands of a satiric and suspicious public. The tragedians of the new era are involved, moreover, in the clichés of technique and afflicted by a general lack of inspiration.

The critics of the eighteenth century turn also to the precepts and critical thought of the preceding century; yet the overthrow of the old order is a certainty, and a growing spirit of change will lead the new theorists to seek other paths. The literary excellence of the ancients, who had endowed the seventeenth century with such a great unity of thought and expression, must now be reevaluated. A new poetics, conforming to the social, political, and artistic demands of the age, is destined to appear.

This study will examine, through a presentation of individual critics of the eighteenth century, the thoughts, attitudes, and theories concerning the genre of tragedy. Of several necessary limitations, the first which has been imposed is that of time: only those figures who produced their criticism during the period from 1714 (a date which approximates the real beginning of the eighteenth century in France, and which coincides with Fénelon's letter to the Académie-Française) until 1799, the date of the appearance of La Harpe's *Lycée,* will be considered. The dramatic judgements of such writers as Crébillon père, Beaumarchais, and Nivelle de la Chaussée will not be examined; for, although these authors are critically articulate, they are recognized primarily as dramatists, and not as critics. Because of the unusually large amount of material, it has been deemed inappropriate to utilize the correspondence of the critics, especially that of Voltaire. In this study, moreover, the reaction of the critics to specific tragedies will be largely ignored, unless the comments and attitudes seem pertinent to a general understanding and interpretation of the genre. Particular attention will be placed on the critics' reaction to the purposé of tragedy, their conception of the rules, their response to the debate over prose and poetry in the tragic theater, their consideration of the validity of love as a suitable dramatic subject, and their concern for elements of revitalization within the genre.

JAMES H. DAVIS, JR.

Athens, Georgia
June 1, 1966

I am indebted to the General Research Fund of the University of Georgia and to Dr. Robert McRorie for assistance in the publication of this work.

TABLE OF CONTENTS

	Page
PREFACE	7

CHAPTER

		Page
I.	The Critics of the Transition: Fénelon, Du Bos, and La Motte.	11
II.	Voltaire and Tragic Theory	30
III.	The Abbé Batteux	44
IV.	Grimm and His View of Tragedy in the *Correspondance Littéraire*	51
V.	Diderot and Tragedy	60
VI.	Marmontel	70
VII.	Louis-Sébastien Mercier	86
VIII.	La Harpe	99
IX.	Conclusion	110

BIBLIOGRAPHY	119

CHAPTER I

CRITICS OF THE TRANSITION: FÉNELON, DU BOS, AND LA MOTTE

François de Salignac de la Mothe-Fénelon, the controversial Archbishop of Cambrai, remembered chiefly for his *Traité de l'éducation des filles* (1687) and for his *Télémaque* (1699), emerges also as a critic on the basis of two documents — the *Dialogues sur l'éloquence* and the *Lettre à M. Dacier sur les occupations de l'Académie*. The second of these works, written in 1714, practically on the eve of his death, falls within the scope of this study. On the strength of its incidental remarks, Saintsbury effusively calls it "the most valuable single piece of criticism that France had yet produced."[1] This report to the French Academy, with its rather brief section on tragedy, is not a document of revolt; it is a prelude to a proposed poetics which could have been filled with stunning reforms.

The part of Fénelon's letter dealing with tragedy is entitled "Projet d'un traité sur la tragédie." He makes a clear distinction between tragedy and comedy by stating that the former represents great events which excite violent passions. Proceeding from this definition, Fénelon launches an attack on certain abuses and on certain poets whom he does not name. These poets are guilty of making tragedies "languissans, fades, et doucereux comme les

---

[1] George E. B. Saintsbury, *A History of Criticism* (New York: Dodd, Mead, and Co., 1902), II, 306. Alfred Lombard also cites a similar opinion, expressed by Professor Schinz and others. See: Lombard, *Fénelon et le retour à l'antique au XVIIIe siècle* (Neuchâtel: Secrétariat de l'Université, 1954), p. 69.

romans," instead of endowing them with "une merveilleuse force, suivant les idées philosophique de l'antiquité, sans y mêler cet amour volage et déréglé qui fait tant de ravages." Even Corneille and Racine, who deserve the greatest praise, have been carried away by the torrent; they have ceded to a taste which is *romanesque*. Fénelon cites, as an example, the episode concerning the love of Dircé for Thésée in Corneille's *Oedipe*, an episode which in his opinion should have been omitted. Likewise, Racine should have presented Phèdre alone in her fury. According to Fénelon, then, the "intrigue galante" has become, and regretfully so, an essential part of tragedy.[2]

There are other abuses which call for remedy. The epigrammatic speeches of tragedy are pompous and affected. Natural speech is what this genre should possess, not a *récit* such as Théramène's. Hippolytus' death could have been reported more effectively with the following words: "Hippolyte est mort. Un monstre envoyé du fond de la mer par la colère des dieux l'a fait périr. Je l'ai vu." Fénelon also broaches the question of rhyme, a question which will so greatly occupy the critics of the eighteenth century. He condemns it as being "gênante," often causing the best tragic poets to "faire des vers chargés d'épithètes pour attraper la rime." In brief, rhyme is a drawback to his idea of naturalness in speech. (XXI, 214-216).

With naturalness Fénelon couples the idea of simplicity. Sophocles' classical restraint and use of "mots entrecoupés" are cited. Racine, our critic tells us, had the plan for an Oedipus play which would have followed the same path as Sophoclean taste. This play could have been "très curieux, très vif, très rapide, très intéressant." We do not find, however, in Corneille's *Cinna* an Augustus who speaks with simplicity, this modest simplicity with which Suetonius depicts him. Besides this latter author, Cicero, Livy, and Plutarch have shown us the lofty Roman; but at the same time, they have revealed to us the Roman who was natural and modest in his speech (XXI, 215-220).

---

[2] François de Salignac de la Mothe Fénelon, *Œuvres* (23 vols.; Paris: J. A. Lebel, 1824), XXI, 212-213. Subsequent citations from Fénelon refer to this edition.

Fénelon's report to Dacier and the Academy is not revolutionary in asking that the excessive use of love in tragedy be reduced. Its attack on rhyme, however, its statements on verbosity and pompousness in tragedy are not to be accepted as common for the era. Significant is the fact that through this letter, Fénelon emerges the champion of the natural and the simple, two elements which will help bring tragedy nearer the grasp of an audience. [3]

Five years after the appearance of the *Lettre sur les occupations,* the Abbé Jean Baptiste Du Bos published his *Réflexions sur la poésie et sur la peinture.* This treatise, which appeared when he was forty-nine, was largely responsible for his election to the French Academy in 1720. [4] Surprisingly, Du Bos' attachment to the church does not lead him to a condemnation of the theater; rather, he is the diplomat-cosmopolite turned critic, who presents a defense of this institution in the midst of formal theories. Poetry and emotion serving as a path to good as well as evil is a principle of volume one of his treatise, but it has been noted that a clear moral idea is lacking in the *Réflexions.* [5] The main concern of Du Bos is the esthetic, the *sentiment* which surrounds all forms of poetry.

Du Bos defines tragedy as

> l'imitation de la vie et du discours des héros ou des hommes sujets par leur élévation aux passions les plus violentes. Elle est l'imitation des crimes et des malheurs des grands hommes; comme des vertus les plus sublimes dont ils soient capables. [6].

The comic poet depicts our friends and shows us people with whom we live everyday, while the tragedian exposes us to the difficulties of sovereigns and other people capable of avenging themselves with splendor. These are the people, then, who are suitable

---

[3] E. B. O. Borgerhoff, *The Evolution of Liberal Theory and Practice in the French Theater (1680-1757)* (Princeton: Princeton University Press, 1936), p. 13.

[4] Alfred Lombard, *L'Abbé Du Bos* (Paris: Hachette, 1913), p. 58.

[5] *Ibid.,* pp. 275-276.

[6] Jean-Baptiste Du Bos, *Réflexions critiques sur la poésie et sur la peinture* (Dresde: Chez George Conrad Walther, 1760), I, 57-58. Further citations refer to this specific edition.

for being depicted, those who can give occasion for the portrayal of great events (I, 55-56).

For Du Bos this concept leads to an elevated idea of tragedy. Here the passions which are more impetuous concern us more than the laughter and scorn found in comedies. Du Bos believes, moreover, that we can bear mediocre tragedy more willingly than mediocre comedy (I, 54; 58). Since tragedy is to excite terror and passion, the people performing it must give it every possible dignity. They must speak in a tone of voice "plus élevé, plus grave, et plus soutenu que celui sur lequel on parle dans les conversations ordinaires." This declamation may be further from truth, but it has more dignity; it is heard better by the spectators (I, 404-405).

Pursuing still the idea of dignity and elevation, Du Bos elaborates on a more exact idea of tragic characters. They must, first, be placed in interesting situations, removed from the possibility of too great familiarity (I, 53). The main character must be amiable and esteemed; he must be shown to us in a state of misfortune. True to Aristotelian precept, Du Bos feels that if we do not esteem him, then we cannot lament his fate. True terror and compassion cannot be evoked in favor of the scoundrel who deserves punishment. Recognizing that there is a penalty to be paid for great crimes, moreover, does not make us fear for ourselves, nor does it win our compassion. But terror and compassion, the two dominating passions, can be heightened for the main character by the use of the villain, the one who violates a "loi naturelle." Phèdre's *confidente* is an example. The main interest of the play, however, must not center about this villainous character. Certain despicable beings should never appear on the stage, namely those who speak against religion (I, 106-112).

Not only must the main characters be interesting, but they must possess *raison*, shaken only by events which would inspire real fear in a courageous man. These characters must be worthy of our veneration, since they will cause us to shed tears. If the tragic character is a contemporary, we are more apt to know his flaws; therefore, it is better to choose the hero "dans des temps éloignés d'une certaine distance du nôtre." (I, 115-119.)

According to Du Bos, the material for tragedy is abundant; and that which does not please one may please another. For him, Corneille and Racine exist as proof of this statement (I, 219 ff.).

The chief aim of the tragic poet, however, is the incorporation of extraordinary incident (which can be original) and the action of characters who are "faits à plaisir" (I, 222).

Vraisemblance should always be maintained by the tragedian. Du Bos' discussion of this classic principle arises when he discourses on the use of historical subjects. In treating historical facts, one may do away with part of the truth, for "un fait vraisemblable est un fait possible dans les circonstances où on le fait arriver." He maintains, following Aristotelian principle, that the false is sometimes more *vraisemblable* than truth. Du Bos believes that a tragic poet sins against his art when he sins too greatly against history, chronology, and geography. One cannot, for example, have Caesar kill Brutus. One should not change anything concerning events, customs, and manners unless there is great necessity for it. Du Bos also cautions against the use of recent history as subject for tragedy. Racine is sharply censured for his *Bajazet* on this basis. The location for this tragedy does not compensate for the fact that there are many who know the customs and uses of the Turks (I, 229-235; 148-149). Everything which has a historical background cannot be staged, for the theater is a book destined to be read in public; it is a book in which *bienséance* must be observed, even with more severity than in history (I, 145).

As observed in Fénelon's letter to the Academy, French tragedy, early in the eighteenth century, was under full attack, both at home and abroad for its presentation of *galanterie* in the guise of love. Here Du Bos approaches the problem, accounting first of all for the use of love as a tragic subject. Poets, he remarks, choose as subjects of their imitations the effects of passions which are the most general; and of all the passions, love is the most general. Our poets, therefore, cannot be blamed for its use in tragedy, if they employ it with reserve and caution. The ancients, according to Du Bos, did not use love as a means to an end so far as tragic composition was concerned. This, also should be avoided by the French. This idea of love as a tragic *ressort* is not founded on truth and is a continual threat to *vraisemblance* (I, 125-126).

To give his compatriots an idea of their mistakes, Du Bos cites the opinion of Wotton, an English critic: the French are guilty of a false depiction of love in their plays. "Galants" are presented to the spectator instead of men who are truly in love. This use of *galanterie,* continues the Englishman, which attempts to reconcile love and reason, is transforming French drama into something close to the burlesque genre (I, 127). Du Bos, no doubt, uses his English critic as a warning, and then turns to remind one that the depiction of love in the writings of the ancients has touched and moved all centuries (I, 136).

Du Bos clearly condemns the use of allegorical material in tragedy, the aim of which is to move us through the imitation of human passions. The author who might use allegory would not be speaking directly to us, and since he, in person, could not explain his allegorical references, we would not understand the work. A dramatic poem which speaks only to the mind could not hold our attention for its duration. Du Bos maintains that allegorical action is suitable only for the prologue to operas which are destined to serve as a type of preface to tragedy (I, 209-213).

As for classical conventions and principles, the section on tragedy in the *Réflexions* considers such elements as versification, *bienséance* or *décence,* the *récit,* and *raison.* To consider the first of these is to know that the *Réflexions* is not a document written against poetry or versification. What Du Bos does, however, is to establish himself firmly, like Fénelon, as an enemy of rhyme. For him, rhyme does not signify the imitation of any beauty which is in nature (I, 69). It is, indeed, a troublesome chain about the neck of the poet whose creation is reduced to nothing more than a mechanical process. This is also due in part to the caesura and the specific number of syllables required for each line (I, 308-309). Latin hexameters are equal in pronunciation, while French alexandrines are very often unequal, although they have uniform progression. The cadence is, however, too uniform. For Du Bos, rhythm and harmony are more important, then, than these other requirements (I, 320-321; 329-335).

Du Bos realizes that *bienséance* and *raison* limit the tragic poet; but, according to him, the laws of tragedy are founded on "bonnes raisons." Since horrible events, such as Brutus and Cassius plunging the dagger into Caesar's heart, can never be presented with *vraisemblance* and *décence,* they degenerate into a performance which is insensitive and childish. The *récit,* recognized here as necessary, also limits the poet, since it is only an imitation of an imitation. Du Bos continues:

> Quoique l'action qu'on nous montre dans un récit pour parler ainsi, soit très touchant par elle-même, elle nous émouvra moins que ne le ferait une autre action moins tragique, mais qui se passerait sous nos yeux et qui serait représentée devant nous dramatiquement (I, 97-98).

Thus we see that Du Bos is far from being a thorough neo-classicist. For him, regularity does not exist for the sake of regularity, nor should it add to the detriment of other qualities which a dramatic creation should possess. We may admire certain plays which are nothing less than regular, but which are supported by an invention and a poetic style "qui de moment en moment présente des images qui nous rendent attentifs et nous émeuvent." We fail to notice the true defects of the play because of certain beauties springing up again and again throughout the work (I, 267). The great masters have not regarded regularity as the final aim of their art, but simply as a means of creating these beauties of a superior order (II, 4).

On the subject of catharsis, Du Bos remarks that poets and painters excite in us artificial passions by presenting imitations of objects capable of exciting real passions within us: "La copie de l'objet doit, pour ainsi dire, exciter en nous une copie de la passion que l'objet y aurait excitée" (I, 25-26). But since the impression which the imitation makes is not as lasting or as serious as the impression which the object itself would have made, it is soon erased from our mind. Our need for agitation has been satisfied, but our tranquility is in danger.

Du Bos' idea of catharsis is linked to his idea of illusion, for he does not believe that illusion is the main cause for the pleasure which we receive from a play. Again it is a question of our seeing a copy. We know beforehand that we will not see the real Chimène, and that we, the spectators, will keep our "bon sens" —even in the midst of most stirring emotion. Excellent dramatic poems can afford us even greater pleasure when we see them for the second time, and when there is no need for further illusion to be created (I, 416-420).

In the *Réflexions* Du Bos establishes *sentiment* as the judge in artistic matters, not *raison* and the rules as Boileau had done some four and a half decades before. Du Bos is not an impressionist or a relativist critic, but he did perhaps pave the way for these ideas of criticism in the nineteenth century.[7] While renovating to a great extent critical practices, he has, at the same time, ignored the fact that the strongest sensations are not always the most artistic.[8]

Antoine Houdar de la Motte (1672-1731), celebrated in the manuals for his polemical relationship with Madame Dacier (which brought about a revival of the Ancients and Moderns controversy in 1713) and as the author of the successful *Inès de Castro* (1723), owed to his Jesuit training a love for the theater. To the society of the cafés of the early eighteenth century he owed his taste for dispute, his penchant to fight established principles, and also his tendency for paradox. Revolt and paradox, indeed, do reign in the period of the regency; and these are the forces which help to throw La Motte from the beaten path and propel him towards a criticism aimed at *nouveauté*.[9]

The dramatic theories of La Motte relative to this study[10] are found in his *Réflexions sur la critique* (1715), in four *discours* (published 1730), in an additional discourse addressed to Voltaire and entitled *Suite des réflexions sur la tragédie*, and in a miscellaneous essay, the *Discours sur le différent mérite des ouvrages d'esprit*. These are the documents, then, which contribute to his hour of celebrity; these works form the substance of the dramatic polemics of this "génie intermédiaire."[11]

The *Réflexions sur la critique* present a general examination of poetic forms with a negligible emphasis on tragedy. Since this document is an answer to Madame Dacier on questions which arose from their dispute over Homer, unity of action here is con-

---

[7] Marcel Braunschvig, *L'Abbé Du Bos. Rénovateur de la critique au XVIIIᵉ siècle* (Toulouse: Librairie Brun, 1904), pp. 23-24.

[8] Lombard, p. 210.

[9] Paul Dupont, *Houdar de la Motte* (Paris: Hachette, 1898), pp. 12-13; 16.

[10] Two earlier items, The *Discours sur la poésie en général* and the *Ode de M. de la Faye*, contain only very brief allusions to tragedy.

[11] Dupont, p. 304.

sidered primarily in connection with the epic. La Motte re-evaluates the definition of art as an imitation of nature by stating that the word *nature* means "une nature choisie, c'est-à-dire, des caractères dignes d'attention, et des objets qui puissent faire des impressions agréables." [12] Imitation cannot be separated from the purpose which the poet has in mind. Epic, tragedy, comedy, the ode, the pastoral, and the satire — all imitate nature, but with different views. Often, says La Motte, a good imitation in one genre will be a very bad one in another.

The *Réflexions* are specific with regard to the pleasure of tragedy and the use of maxims in this genre. There are two pleasures to be derived from the representation of a tragedy. The first stems from the very fact that one is participating in an important action which is taking place for the first time before our eyes. We become agitated by the fear and by the hope which the characters create. We share their happiness or their misfortune, according to their eventual triumph or defeat; through "surprises pathétiques," terror and pity are evoked. The second pleasure is explained as "la vue de l'art même que l'auteur a employé pour exciter le premier" (III, 110-111).

The long *maxime* or *sentence* is attacked by La Motte. It has a chilling effect on the *pathétique*, for passion disavows the extensive and raving maxim. Racine, he points out, knew how to cover the maxim [13] "sous un sentiment direct; ce qui sans rien faire perdre au lecteur de la vérité générale, a l'air plus naturel et plus animé" (III, 224-225).

In his first discourse, accompanying his tragedy *Les Machabées*, which had been presented in 1721, La Motte praises *nouveauté*, for here he is the proponent of innovation in action as well as the advocate of grandeur of action (IV, 26-27). This innovation leads him to speak of material and subject matter for tragedy. Some material affords the author only one scene. The poet actually needs to imagine multiplying circumstances which place the same character and the same virtue under various tests of

---

[12] Houdar de la Motte, *Œuvres* (10 vols.; Paris: Chez Prault, 1754), III, 106-107; 188-189.
[13] La Motte also attacks the use of the long maxim in his *Discours sur l'églogue*, III, 314. He discourses further on the maxim in his *Troisième discours*, IV, 297-302.

strength so that he may maintain this passion which he has proposed to excite in us (IV, 30-31).

Love is established as a necessary element in tragedy, despite the fact that the French have been criticized for placing it in tragedies whose subjects show resistance to it. The dramatist wishes to succeed and can do so only by pleasing an audience composed mainly of women. Love is a subject which will move them; love is, moreover, the greatest passion which will affect this sex. Thus in using love, the dramatist, according to La Motte, thinks more of success than of perfection. Love is, however, a natural passion, general enough not to be foreign in any place. He suggests that love be combined with other passions, with other interests, with other characters. Let other causes be linked to it so that one does not see lovers in general. Let specific men in love be seen (IV, 31-34).

The *Premier discours* considers the three unities and introduces the idea of a fourth, without which the other three are declared useless. This essential unity is that of interest, and it is "la vraie source de l'émotion continue." The unity of action is the most fundamental; but it is not, however, the same as the unity of interest. If, for example, several characters are involved in the same event, and if they all are worthy of your attention, there is, La Motte agrees, a unity of action. There is, however, no unity of interest present; for in order to follow the progress of certain characters, you are inclined to lose sight of the others (IV, 44).

La Motte attacks both the unities of time and place. It is not natural that every single part of the action take place in an *appartement* or in the same public square. Only by chance would you be able to assemble different characters in one location. Despite the resources of art, the greatest poets "violent bien des convenances pour satisfaire à cette règle prétendue." Suppression of the unity of place will not make the action any less true, and actually, the ignoring of it may cause the illusion to become stronger. It is, therefore, a "unité forcée", which often deprives the spectator of certain actions which he would like to see, and which can only be revealed to him through a less impressive *récit* (IV, 38-40).

The unity of time is no more reasonable, and especially if it is pushed to the same extreme as the unity of place. Even with the convenient extension which allows the poet to use twenty-four hours instead of only the time required for presentation, there remain subjects which could not be reduced to this limit without harming them. Thus La Motte speaks strongly against these two unities, but at the same time makes it clear that he does not want to abolish them. It is simply a matter of not adhering to them with superstition, in order that more essential beauties may be produced. The rules are far from useless:

> Je conviens qu'elles forment un art; et leur première utilité, c'est que la contrainte qu'elles imposent, détourne de la carrière des esprits médiocres qui ne craindraient pas d'y entrer, si elle était plus libre. C'est proprement la pierre de touche du talent nécessaire (IV, 41-43).

The rules, when observed, compose a great part of our pleasure; we recognize the difficulty in preparing these works which please us because they are *raisonnable*.

La Motte's consideration of versification constitutes the subject matter for the last part of the *Premier discours*. He recognizes it as an essential part of tragedy. It is an art which has essentially simple laws if regarded as "l'art de captiver son sens sous une action contrainte." In versification one must consider simply the regularity of rhymes, *enjambement,* the number of required syllables, and the hemistich. Versification, moreover, must be clear, thereby avoiding violent transpositions, equivocal terms, and a profusion of figures. It must be noble, a quality which depends on thought and expression. This nobility involves simplicity on certain occasions. Versification must be suitable to the characters, the material, and the situations. The application of this principle accounts for differences in style which becomes either sublime, heroic, pathetic, or simple (IV, 51-56).

La Motte will accept no idea of *nouveauté* so far as the alexandrine is concerned. In a resigned fashion, he admits that this verse form is in possession of tragedy, despite the fact that *vers libres* are even closer to prose. La Motte reminds us that Corneille attempted this free verse in his *Agésilas,* but unsuccessfully. Perhaps an excellent play could have created a vogue for this type of verse, but innovation at the present time would be dangerous.

In his discourse accompanying *Romulus* (presented in 1722), La Motte answers his critics who attack the multiplicity of events in the play. The advantage of simplicity lies in the fact that it requires only the slight attention of the spectator, thus permitting him to become more involved in the passion of the drama, and freeing him from the trouble of disentangling certain circumstances. Simplicity does not, however, exercise the imagination enough; and this can be remedied by presenting the same object in different lights, in different guises. Multiplicity, then, leads the mind from object to object, renewing its curiosity, and continually adding to the emotions of the heart.

If there is a danger in this multiplicity, it would stem from the fact that there is confusion. The play would no longer be entertainment, but what La Motte calls an "étude." This pitfall can be avoided by having an order to the events, and by having them dependent on one interest. Our critic advocates a type of multiplicity where "l'esprit et le cœur sont émus à tout moment par des tableaux variés, et qu'ainsi et la curiosité et la passion y sont à la fois et plus sûrement satisfaites" (IV, 150-151).

The *Second discours* presents a discussion of exposition and dramatic situation. The former, according to La Motte, lays the foundation for the play and establishes the character of the tragic actors. Tragedy is an action, says the critic, and thus the poet must be hidden; the audience must not notice that it is the author who arranges the ways and means. The spectators must not know that it is the poet who is using his characters to his advantage (IV, 153). The exposition of a tragedy should be incorporated into the action, for the whole tragedy should be action, and, if possible, the first scene as well as the others (IV, 155-156).

Nouveauté, one of La Motte's guiding principles in his dramatic criticism, is again advocated if one is to show situations in tragedy with great effect. To this is added what he calls "the importance of interests." An illustration of this idea is furnished by recalling the scene from Act five of *Rodogune*. Here Antiochus prepares to drink from the nuptial cup amid suspicions of its being poisoned. The surprise is maintained and renewed throughout the scene, successful because of its curiosity and interest.

The *discours* of the characters are not foretold, and our attention is drawn to the various movements of son, mother, and princess (IV, 158-160).

Recognition scenes help to form situations for the dramatic author; but the true idea of recognition for La Motte involves the reunion of two people, separated for a long time, who finally recognize each other through questions asked and details related. The exclamations which follow are almost sure to bring forth our tears. The recognition scene should not degenerate into "longs discours sur l'état présent des choses," unless the dramatist is prepared to furnish the spectator with speeches as *pathétique* as the situation itself (IV, 161-163).

In discussing tragic characters, La Motte divides them into three categories— "naturels, intéressants, et soutenus." Characters must be natural because one would prefer to recognize mankind throughout the work. Corneille's *Pertharite* failed because of the strangeness of its characters and its *sentiments*. Mathan in *Athalie*, for example, is an excessive, odious character; he cannot be natural. Even if history furnishes us with such a character, there can be no justification for his place in the theater, where one prefers to see men and not monsters (IV, 165-167).

Interesting characters can be considered as such only in the following ways: through a virtue which is perfect; through imposing qualities, which give the idea of virtue and greatness; through the grouping of both virtues and weaknesses in a character. La Motte admits, however, that a completely virtuous character is a rarity, while a character who is a mixture of vice and virtue is admired less, but in the end evokes our compassion (IV, 172). Our pride is flattered in seeing faults linked to great qualities; and this combat of passion and virtue, this agitation, "ce sont ces secousses de l'âme qui font précisément le plaisir de la tragédie" (IV, 176-177).

What La Motte means by a "caractère soutenu" is explained in terms of Aristotelian consistency, for characters should not contradict themselves; and one particular action cannot be fitted to a single quality if the rest of the man's character is opposed to it. Characters such as Medea and Cleopatra (in *Rodogune*), who are only partly odious, can be used with success. This idea leads La Motte to speak of tragedy as a school of vice and virtue.

He feels that in tragedy there is only an indirect instruction. In an odious character, we see, for example, the horror of the crime weakened by worthy motives and by great misfortunes which tend to excuse him. In certain cases the guilty characters are found to be more unfortunate at the end of the play than the ones oppressed (IV, 178-182).

The last section of this second discourse is a plea for the use of pomp, display, and spectacle in tragedy. Most French plays are considered by La Motte to be only dialogues and *récits;* the impressive action takes place behind the scenes. There are, of course, certain actions which are not intended for the eyes — both horrible events and those elements difficult to stage. Since our minds are more readily impressed through our eyes than through our ears, action should replace the *récit.* The very presence of actors will be more effective than the most carefully written *récit* (IV, 183-187).

La Motte's *Troisième discours à l'occasion de la tragédie d'Inès* is interesting for the critic's ideas on conjugal love in the tragedy; for his comments on the pleasure of tragedy; for his views on the use of *confidents,* monologues, and maxims. The conflicts of conjugal love are deemed worthy elements of tragedy, but poets are urged to place married couples in situations strong enough to unfold passion which should be felt more keenly than the duty which exists between the two (IV, 266-267).

One cause for pleasure in tragedy stems from the fact that the action, from the very beginning, is carried to a high point of interest; and this interest grows without interruption until the end of the play. The dramatist is warned about the delay in exciting the first emotions, for there are too many tragedies with acts lost in preparations. Sometimes because of lack of *invention* or subject, tragedies become half-tragedies. Pity and fear, essential elements of tragic pleasure, must be excited in every act (IV, 271-273). La Motte speaks again of this gradation in his *Discours sur le différent mérite des ouvrages d'esprit.* Here it is a question of arranging beauty in an order which can give the desired effect:

> Cette méthode est particulièrement nécessaire aux poètes dramatiques, qui quelquefois avec autant d'esprit et de beautés qu'il en faut pour réussir, ne laissent pas de

tomber par le seul défaut d'économie. Ils pourroient presque toujours se répondre du succès, s'ils sçavoient reculer les grandes beautés jusqu'aux derniers actes, et observer cette gradation dans chaque acte en particulier, et même jusques dans chaque scène (VIII, 362).

Since *confidents,* according to La Motte, have no real part in the action of a tragedy, except to allow the hero to catch his breath, he calls them "personnages surabondants." If there are too many of these useless characters in a play, then the progress of the tragedy is suspended. He does not include Phoenix and Oenone in this category, since they are only half-*confidents* and not certain cold, colorless characters which one is likely to see. Perhaps there is a means of constructing a tragedy in which a *confident* could be made to act by reserving for him some personal passion which might influence the decisions of the main roles; but for the present, La Motte boasts of the *nouveauté* of his *Inès de Castro,* which presents no *confident* (IV, 277-279).

The dramatic poet should use the least possible number of monologues in composing his tragedy, since "quelques résolutions brusques en font une matière plus naturelle et plus raisonnable" (IV, 280-283). Frequent interruptions are needed in the dialogue to inspire its greatest perfection which is vivacity. This element is as necessary to dialogue as action is to tragedy. Maxims, moreover, add nothing to dialogue; they only tend to make it less natural and less true. Tragic characters are almost always agitated by violent passions and are not meant to speak a type of general reflexion. If they do so, then they become *raisonneurs* instead of people whom we should admire or pity. When used, maxims should be rapid, filling a place where reasoning and thought are appropriate (IV, 297-302).

La Motte attempts to show the advantages of the prose tragedy in a fourth discourse, written as a companion piece to his *Oedipe,* a play which had been presented in 1726. [14] He acknowledges the fact that the practice of composing tragic works in verse is well established, that the pomp and measure of verse are essential to

---

[14] La Motte actually wrote two versions of *Œdipe* — one in verse, one in prose.

tragedy, that terror and the *pathétique* would not be produced from the effect of ordinary language. He also reminds the reader that the actor would be abashed if deprived of his verse recitation which aids his acting intelligence, and which helps him to achieve better tones. These are prejudices established by custom and maintained through prudence.

Advantages to prose tragedies can be shown, however; and the first of these is *vraisemblance*, which is violated by versification. With ordinary language, *sentiment* would appear more real and true; this would apply to action also. The tragic character should speak more nobly and more elegantly than comic ones, but he should not speak less naturally. The dignity of a tragic character does not make him a poet. Therefore, there is an advantage to prose, since it will grant the dramatist more liberty to choose and arrange words; he will be endowed with greater facility to correct and then perfect his creation. La Motte laments the fact that many potential tragic poets are lost to this art through discouragement at the amount of time required to write in verse (IV, 390-396). Like Boileau, La Motte realizes the tyranny of rhyme. He calls it "le hasard des rimes" and comments on the fact that the bad poet is the slave of this "chance" (IV, 411).

For La Motte the unattractive, unnecessary parts of poetry are "les expressions audacieuses, les figures hyperboliques," all this language deprived of ordinary usage. The great merit of Racine's poetry lies in the fact that here there is no search for the ornamental and the audacious. These elements are reserved for the orator. The dramatic author should be faithful to his characters and to the passions which he represents, imitating as closely as possible the natural speech of important people (IV, 413-415).

In response to Voltaire's preface to his own *Oedipe* (1730), La Motte composed a *Suite des réflexions sur la tragédie où l'on répond à M. de Voltaire*. His main concerns here are a further examination of the question of poetry [15] and a further elaboration

---

[15] The Abbé Desfontaines (1685-1746), minor critic and friend to Fréron, added his views to those of Voltaire and La Motte in his *Nouvelliste du Parnasse* (Paris: Chez Chaubert, 1734). He states that La Motte's ideas on tragedy are new and original, but that he cannot permit that he take rhyme away from poetry. Desfontaines also says that French poets should observe the essential laws of the theater. Perhaps there is a possibility of a

of his ideas on the unities. As for poetry, La Motte attempts to draw a line between it and what he calls "vers." He maintains that he is not speaking against "poésie," and that if verse were denied to men of genius, some writers would still be able to be poets in prose (IV, 423-424).

Before presenting additional reflexions on the unities, La Motte censures dramatic authors of the preceding century for their ignorance of what he calls "les sources immédiates du plaisir." Racine did, however, find a new direction in *Andromaque;* here the actors are placed in situations which are animated and alive. The characters are less like *raisonneurs*. Here the true aim and the real pleasure of the tragedy were achieved; tears were drawn from the spectator (IV, 426-427).

To defend himself against the reproaches of Voltaire, La Motte emphatically asserts his loyalty to the unities. He has, if we believe him, been as faithful as the great masters. The restraints of the theater which he has elucidated, the reforms which he has proposed are for the instruction of his successors — even for Voltaire himself. This statement helps to account for La Motte's paradoxical ramblings between the realms of theory and practice. Here he admits the usefulness of the unities, stressing again that the unity of action is fundamental. The unities remain, however, independent of one another (IV, 430).

The unity of interest, mentioned in the *Premier discours,* and more sharply defined here in the *Suite des réflexions,* is independent of the other three. Corneille's *Le Cid* illustrates the fact that a play can possess the unity of interest and at the same time ignore the other three, for the unity of interest is not the same as the unity of action. Corneille's *Oedipe,* for example, has a single action: the search for the murderer of Laius. There are, nonetheless, two interests in the play. In the first place, we are

---

tragedy in prose, but for the moment he agrees with Voltaire, the defender of poetry. In works of the imagination, versification is superior to prose. According to Desfontaines, La Motte is justified in censuring the alexandrine. A new manner of versification could be invented "sans rimes et sans hémistiches, avec la seule mesure des mots, jointe au mélange, des syllabes longues et brèves que nous avons, et des différentes terminaisons, pour varier l'harmonie, et flatter l'oreille." At any rate, prosaic language is too cold and too commonplace (pp. 26; 200-204).

concerned with Theseus who is accused of the crime; subsequently, the danger falls upon Oedipus himself. Voltaire, likewise, uses much the same technique in his version by having Philoctetes first accused before passing to a condemnation of Oedipus. La Motte reminds us, however, that in his own *Oedipe,* the peril which comes to Oedipus' children is directly connected to his own misfortune.

Not only must there be a single interest, but it must be "grand, continu," increasing as the play progresses. The interest can be uninterrupted, thus continuing through "la présence fréquente des personnages pour qui le spectateur a pris parti." It is better, in other words, to see the actors rather than to hear them described. It is also better to have the interest fall on two people who fear each other (IV, 431-438).

La Motte is a *moderne,* but his works are classic in form. Demanding *nouveauté* throughout his critical work, he is more indulgent with regard to his own dramatic creations.[16] There is a timidity of execution in his tragedies, and this timidity is even more astonishing when one compares them to the *discours.*[17] What he proposes to do — and his reforms are bold for the era — and what he actually does constitute a sort of paradox:

> Il a introduit le spectacle dans son *Romulus,* mais prudemment. Il a donné place à l'amour conjugal dans *Inès* malgré le préjugé. Dans *Œdipe,* il a cherché à appliquer ses idées assez confuses sur l'unité d'intérêt. Un peu partout, il s'est efforcé timidement d'intéresser les confidents à l'action, de réduire les monologues et les récits. Mais il n'a guère réussi parce que, tout en proclamant la nécessité d'une action rapide, il s'est bien gardé d'appliquer résolument les principes qu'il posait.[18]

La Motte, as a transitional critic, was influenced by the *geomètres,* whose meetings brought about an exchange of ideas and affected the minds of even the poets. La Motte was touched, at least in part, by their insensibility to literary prejudice. He has

---

[16] Dupont, p. 72.
[17] *Ibid,* p. 58.
[18] *Ibid.,* p. 275.

the thankless role of closing a great century and of opening a great century; [19] his critical work remains a legacy, a guidebook for his successors.

---

[19] Dupont, pp. 13-14; 303.

Chapter II

VOLTAIRE AND TRAGIC THEORY

François-Marie Arouet de Voltaire, striding across the genres like a colossus, dominates the second generation of writers in the eighteenth century, just as Crébillon père and Houdar de la Motte had reigned over the first.[1] The critical work of Voltaire is multiple and scattered throughout all aspects of his work. We find it in certain articles of his *Dictionnaire philosophique,* in the notes for a tragedy, in the corner of an *épître* or a *stance,* throughout the voluminous correspondence, in the literary chapters of his historical studies, and even in various polemical items, such as the *Eloge de Crébillon.* Although it is a body of material through which Voltaire is not best known today as a critic, his dramatic criticism constitutes his real poetics. It is found mainly in the *préfaces* and *dédicaces* to his plays, but also in the *Commentaire sur Corneille,* perhaps his greatest critical undertaking; in an article entitled "Art Dramatique," which appears in the *Dictionnaire philosophique;* in the *Appel à toutes les nations,* a miscellaneous essay; and in his 1776 letter to the French Academy.[2]

We shall begin by considering the dramatic criticism of Voltaire's formative period, which we might designate as 1719-1736. The *Lettres sur Oedipe* of 1719 are an examination of his own play in terms of the creations of Sophocles and Corneille. Voltaire shows, no doubt, his ignorance of things Greek, but his reproaches against Sophocles bring to light, for example, his admiration for

---

[1] Raymond Naves, *Le Goût de Voltaire* (Paris: Garnier, 1938), p. 358.
[2] *Ibid.,* pp. 186-188.

vraisemblance and certain of his ideas on simplicity in the theater. According to Voltaire, Sophocles sins against *vraisemblance* by having Oedipus know nothing of his predecessor.[3] If a chorus is used, it must be presented with *vraisemblance*, as seen in Racine's *Athalie* (II, 43). The art of the theater requires at all times this classic principle. Voltaire recognizes the simplicity of the Greek theater, but he feels that it possesses what he terms "sécheresse." This is a disturbing element for the dramatist of the present who does not find enough expanse nor development here to justify a play of five acts. *Invention,* therefore, is necessary, but secondary episodes, such as the Thésée-Dircé episode in Corneille's *Oedipe,* should be well linked to the main subject (II, 29).

The major reform advocated in this preface is more freedom in rhyme. The word *terre,* for example, should be allowed to rhyme with *mère.* French poetry, says Voltaire, would gain much with new rhymes; new thoughts would be given to authors, and certainly, thought is preferable to rhyme (II, 41). The chief innovation of Voltaire's *Oedipe,* according to the author himself, is his use of the chorus, which acts as a character. Sometimes it appears without speaking, simply for the sake of interest, but also to add pomp to the tragedy. With the ancients, the chorus filled the interval between acts, and this sometimes caused tiring repetition or revealed what was to follow. Voltaire does not see practicality in the continual presence of a chorus, although the ancients looked on it as the foundation of their tragedy (II, 42).

The preface to *Mariamne* in 1725 is characterized by Voltaire's conformity to established principles and practices, and by his condescension to the taste of the public. One must depict heroes as the public imagines them, "car il est bien plus aisé de mener les hommes par les idées qu'ils ont qu'en voulant leur en donner de nouvelles." Therefore the disagreeable characters must be softened, for it is necessary to think of your public even more than your hero. Here also, as early as 1725, Voltaire recognizes the need for action in tragedy and gives preference to it over *récit.* He would have liked for Mariamne to die on the stage "en

---

[3] François-Marie Arouet de Voltaire, *Œuvres complètes,* ed. L. Moland (52 vols.; Paris: Garnier, 1879), II, 19. Subsequent citations refer to this edition.

action" but the *récit*, telling of her demise,[4] conforms to the taste of the public (II, 162-164).

Not until 1730 does Voltaire feel the real need to defend verse in tragedy. He simply tries, at this point, to show the importance of dramatic poetry in relation to superior tragic composition. The alexandrines must be full of strength and harmony, and there must be a continuous elegance in the lines if boredom is to be avoided. Racine, Voltaire's example of perfection, is after Virgil the one who has best known the art of verse (II, 165).

The preface to the 1730 edition of *Oedipe* defends poetry and the unities against the attack of La Motte. Voltaire becomes the definite neo-classicist, stating that all the arts such as tragedy have their roots in *nature* and in *raison*. The rules have guided the great masters — Corneille, Racine, Molière — and he, Voltaire, will observe them, not because they are ancient laws, but because they are good and necessary ones.

Voltaire calls the unities, "sages règles du théâtre." They are essential and joined one to the other. A tragedy is, in effect, a presentation of one action and should be so, since "l'esprit humain ne peut embrasser plusieurs objets à la fois; c'est que l'intérêt qui se partage s'anéantit bientôt." The unity of place is also necessary, "car une seule action ne peut se passer en plusieurs lieux à la fois." At this point the painter and the dramatist become analogous for Voltaire, who reminds us that Le Brun did not paint Alexander both in Arbela and in India on the same canvas (II, 48-49). The unity of time is consequently joined to the other two and naturally so. Voltaire's defense of this principle is based on the fact that one goes to the theater to see a single event in the hero's life, not his complete history. Since a performance lasts for only three hours, the action, then, must not last any longer than this period of time (II, 50).

Voltaire dismisses La Motte's unity of interest, considering it simply as another term for the unity of action. One will find in the best French tragedies that the main characters are "diversement intéressés; mais ces intérêts divers se rapportent tous à celui du

---

[4] We recall the fact that Mariamne did expire before the eyes of the *parterre* in the first performance.

personnage principal, et alors il y a unité d'action." Before leaving this topic, Voltaire cites Corneille's definition of this unity which states that it "consiste en l'unité d'intrigue et en l'unité de péril" (II, 51-52).

Voltaire is shocked that La Motte would write against poetry, for in practice he has given approval to this convention. Here in the preface to *Oedipe*, rhyme is defended on the basis of its being natural to man, existing even among the savage peoples. The ancients honored verse, if not rhyme, and had Virgil been born in Paris, he would have written in rhyme. Versification is not mechanical and ridiculous work as La Motte has said. It may be laborious work, but its great merit stems from the fact that it is as correct as prose and shows at the same time "une difficulté surmontée" (II, 53-55).

The influence of Voltaire's sojourn in England (1726-1729), and his consequent familiarity with English drama are reflected in the prefaces to *Brutus, Eriphyle, La Mort de César*, in the *épîtres dédicatoires* preceding *Zaïre*, and in the well-known *Lettres philosophiques*. In the first of these prefaces, the "Discours sur la tragédie" (1731), which accompanies the *Brutus*, Voltaire vaunts his knowledge of the English language and its great influence over him. It makes him aware of the severity of French poetry and of the "esclavage de la rime." The Frenchman is, indeed, a slave of rhyme, "obligé de faire quelquefois quatre vers pour exprimer une pensée qu'un anglais peut rendre en une seule ligne." But despite this, rhyme is essential to French poetry. With more detail than in the 1730 preface, Voltaire explains why:

> Notre langue ne comporte que peu d'inversions; nos vers ne souffrent point d'enjambement, du moins cette liberté est très rare; nos syllabes ne peuvent produire une harmonie sensible par leurs mesures longues ou brèves; nos césures et un certain nombre de pieds ne suffiraient pas pour distinguer la prose d'avec la versification (II, 312).

Voltaire states definitively that tragedy in prose cannot succeed and that, furthermore, to the demands of rhyme and versification the French owe the excellent works which exist in their language.

Lion has pointed out that in this preface to *Brutus,* Voltaire attacks the French theater for the first time.[5] French tragedies are accused of being conversations rather than the presentations of an event. Here in reality is a cry for action, action which is suppressed by *usage,* convention, and the physical handicap of having the *bancs* on the stage (II, 314-315). If the English and the Greeks have at times passed the limits of *bienséance,* then the French have not attained real tragedy through the fear that they might pass these limits (II, 318). The horrible and the terrible could be presented with art. In the preface to *Eriphyle* (1732), our critic emphasizes again that terror should re-appear in French tragedy (II, 458). Voltaire has seen the great effect produced by the ghost in *Hamlet,* and now he advocates such a device which would give a desired violence of emotion.[6] There is another suggestion stated in the *épître dédicatoire* of *Zaïre* (1733). Voltaire says that he owes to the English theater his boldness of placing on the stage the names of French kings and ancient families of the kingdom. For him this is *nouveauté* and the source for a type of tragedy heretofore unknown in France (II, 542). Voltaire does, in fact, use the names St. Louis and Montmorency in the play.[7]

In the period of English influence, the dramatic criticism of Voltaire shows keen interest in the question of love, *galanterie, tendresse,* and their place in tragedy. The latter part of the *discours* preceding *Brutus* contains Voltaire's answer to the charge that the French have weakened their theater by the presence of too much *tendresse.* He maintains that "vouloir de l'amour dans toutes les tragédies me paraît un goût efféminé; l'en proscrire toujours est une mauvaise humeur bien déraisonnable." The theater whether tragic or comic is "la peinture vivante des passions humaines." Therefore, love is not to be rejected unless it is badly handled or treated without art. Voltaire does admit that love in tragedy is often only *galanterie,* and this quality makes it defective. In order that love be worthy of the tragic theater, it must be "le nœud nécessaire de la pièce," not introduced into the action with constraint and force. It must be, moreover, a truly tragic passion,

---

[5] Henri Lion, *Les Tragédies et les théories dramatiques de Voltaire* (Paris: Hachette, 1895), p. 47.

[6] *Ibid.,* pp. 66-67.

[7] *Ibid.,* p. 71.

leading to misfortune and crime if it is to be seen as dangerous. It can be shown invincible when virtue triumphs over it. Otherwise you will present a type of love suitable only for comedy or eclogue (II, 322-324).

In the second *épître dédicatoire* for Zaïre (1736), Voltaire defends and praises the French treatment of love: "L'amour paraît sur nos théâtres avec des bienséances, une délicatesse, une vérité qu'on ne trouve point ailleurs. C'est que de toutes les nations, la française est celle qui a le plus connu la société." *Tendresse* cannot be achieved through the use of rhetorical hyperboles and *indécences*, such as one sees in Dryden. *Bienséance* is a guiding factor; it is also a rule which the French understand (II, 551-552). In the preface to *La Mort de César*, however, Voltaire speaks against the "intrigue de galanterie." Unfortunately no one dares cure the French theater of this infection which was present even in the works of Corneille and Racine (III, 310).

This first group of critical items reflects Voltaire's respect for the rules and manifests his willingness to follow the "route commune" of French tragedy.[8] In 1730 the unities are the "sages règles," and in 1731 they are the "règles fondamentales" (II, 319). Number eighteen of the *Lettres philosophiques* recognizes the genius of Shakespeare, but remarks that it is genius without good taste or knowledge of the rules. Although he may admit that in English plays there are "lueurs étonnantes," Voltaire must still comment on the fact that English drama is barbarous, deprived of *bienséance*, order, and *vraisemblance* (XXII, 152-153). In the 1733 *épître* preceding Zaïre, he requires that a tragedy possess not only the classical *vérité*, but the ancient simplicity (II, 539). Combined with the one great merit of the English theater — action — these elements, in Voltaire's scheme of things, can lead to new horizons and to new pleasures in the theater without, however, shocking the public.[9]

The dramatic criticism of Voltaire which appeared during the years 1744-1753, and which we assign to the second division of this study, mirrors his continued interest in love as a subject for tragedy. The letter to Scipion Maffei, preceding *Mérope*,

---

[8] *Ibid.*, p. 33.
[9] Naves, p. 146.

praises the Italian nobleman for his *Merope* of 1713. Here is a tragedy worthy of the finest days of the Athenian dramatists, a tragedy in which there is no *galanterie*. One cannot blame Racine, however, for this dominating taste for love in tragedy; in fact, it was he who tried to reform the taste of the nation. Love as a passion is never episodic in Racine, Voltaire reminds the reader; it becomes the foundation of his plays and forms the principal interest in them. To use love, we must know then its limitations:

> C'est la passion la plus théâtrale de toutes, la plus fertile en sentiments, la plus variée: elle doit être l'âme d'un ouvrage de théâtre, ou en être entièrement bannie. Si l'amour n'est pas tragique, il est insipide; et s'il est tragique, il doit régner seul; il n'est pas fait pour la seconde place (IV, 180-182).

This is the same idea we see in the preface to *Brutus* and here restated. To this Voltaire adds his censure not only of the English theater for its misuse of love in tragedy, but also of Corneille and Rotrou for their "intrigues galantes" (IV, 184).

The *épître* to the Duchesse du Maine, which serves as a preface to Voltaire's *Oreste* (1750), repeats basically the same attitude and thoughts concerning love in tragedy. Here the critic requires that love appear as the dominating tyrant — or not at all. For Voltaire there is no place for a love interest in the treatment of the Oedipus legend and certainly no room for *galanterie*, which has its place in comedy and in tales. Love is not worthy of the grandeur of tragedy. Voltaire therefore states that the *Oreste*, which he is offering, is his idea of a tragedy without love, *confidents*, or episodes. He would like to prove that it is possible to maintain Greek subjects without the use of amorous intrigue and romantic adventure (IV, 85-87).

In the preface to his comedy *Nanine* (1749), Voltaire again speaks of love in tragedy, this time as it is seen in good tragedy: "l'amour furieux, barbare, funeste, suivi de crimes et de remords." It is not the tender and naive love which is the mainspring of comedy. Here also is the idea that terror and pity are the soul of tragedy, not love as it is treated in the comic genre (IV, 6). The familiar tone which love takes, moreover, is the point at which tragedy is lowered and comedy is elevated (IV, 9).

In 1753, as a phase of his rivalry with Crébillon, Voltaire presented his *Rome sauvée*. One of his grievances against Crébillon was his use of the "intrigue amoureuse," [10] and in the preface to this play, he informs us that he has wished to write a tragedy "sans déclaration d'amour," a tragedy that would help destroy the reproaches of all Europe against the French for their use of *galanterie* (V, 210). In *Rome sauvée* Voltaire shows the effort of making a historical tragedy from available material, substituting for love a faithful depiction of the mores of that time, a true representation of the character and genius of Catalina, Caesar, and Cato (V, 210). As a matter of evolution, we see that in Voltaire's poetics, the concern for historical mores and the desire for more pomp and spectacle are becoming more apparent.

The *Dissertation sur la tragédie ancienne et moderne* (1749), which precedes *Sémiramis*, reflects Voltaire's shift of interest from things English to an examination of Greek dramatic elements. Voltaire's mounting interest in spectacle is revealed when he asks where one can find an equivalent of the spectacle of the Greek stage. Perhaps only in Italian opera does this image subsist (V, 489). As for nature, the French, beginning with Mairet and the *Sophonisbe*, imitated it in a truer fashion than did the Greeks in their plays. What they could have learned from the moderns in France is the art of clever exposition and the liaison of scenes. In a writer such as Racine, they would have been astonished at the shock of passions, surprised by these well-handled discourses between rivals (IV, 494-495).

This *dissertation* analyzes the question of invention in the tragedy. More frequently than the Greeks did the moderns imagine their own subjects. This does not mean, says Voltaire, that the human heart cannot be moved by this sort of fiction. A subject of pure fiction and a true subject unknown to the spectator are one and the same thing. The person viewing a play cannot consult all the books in question before knowing whether or not he is seeing fable or history, and in the end, he is moved by an effective play. Plays of invention, moreover, are more difficult to write; these imagined characters are harder to create. In fact, it is to some

---

[10] Lion, pp. 214-215.

degree through this *invention* that the French rise above the Greeks in dramatic art (IV, 496-497).

The attractive elements of the Greek theater inspire in Voltaire's criticism a need for certain reforms in French tragedy. He wishes, for example, to equal the ancients in the dignity of their presentation; but the great and moving action of the French theater is hampered by the crowd of spectators confounded with the actors on the stage. From this point, a digression leads Voltaire to mention the bad taste in French décor, the indecency of the *parterre*, the need for better theaters with improved acoustics. The stage is too narrow, since the actors have little more than ten feet in which to move. This fact accounts in part for Voltaire's feeling that the majority of French plays are no more than long conversations. Theatrical action is lacking, an action which he explains in the following way:

> Quand je parle d'une action théâtrale, je parle d'un appareil, d'une cérémonie, d'une assemblée, d'un événement nécessaire à la pièce, et non pas de ces vains spectacles plus puérils que pompeux, de ces ressources du décorateur qui suppléent à la stérilité du poète, et qui amusent les yeux quand on ne sait parler à l'oreille et à l'âme (IV, 499-500).

Voltaire's idea of display and pomp does not, for example, include the idea of having a horse on stage, nor does it advocate the array of a fireworks demonstration (IV, 500-503). Action, color, and ceremonious elements remain important for Voltaire, but it is well to remember his veneration of the simplicity of the Greeks, which he had expressed in the dedication to *Oreste*: "C'était là le vrai caractère de l'invention et du génie; c'était l'essence du théâtre" (IV, 87).

Voltaire's comments on versification, found in the letter preceding *Mérope*, deserve mention here. He attributes the failure of Jean de la Chapelle's *Mérope* (1683) to the coldness of its versification, a vice, as he says, which causes so many dramatic poems to perish. The art of being eloquent in verse is the rarest and most difficult of all the arts; it is a talent given to only three or four men on earth. In this same letter (1744), Voltaire discards the idea of using blank verse, which he does admit, however, possesses facility. Such an attempt would have no success in France (IV, 190).

The critical prefaces and dedications which appeared from 1755 until Voltaire's death in 1778, and which constitute the third division for examination, reflect, first of all, his view that tragedy should depict the mores and customs of other times and other lands. Prior to 1755, we recall that he had presented *Alzire*, which transported the spectator to South America; *Zulime*, which conveyed to the stage a setting in North Africa; *Mahomet*, which left the theater a flavor of the Orient. Now in the *épître dédicatoire* to *L'Orphelin de la Chine*, Voltaire finally elucidates his position with regard to tragedy and mores: "Les aventures les plus intéressantes ne sont rien quand elles ne peignent pas les moeurs ..." (V, 299). As late as 1767, he indicates in the preface to *Les Scythes* that the *nouveauté* of this tragedy is the depiction of mores, "qu'on n'avait point encore exposées sur le théâtre tragique." He is maintaining, as he did in 1749, that tragedies based on material other than historical subjects can be treated with success. There must be, however, something new in these depictions so that the work will not be simply an imitation. For this reason he has presented *nouveauté* which includes a view of medieval knighthood *(Tancrède)*, a contrast of Mohammedans and Christians *(Zaïre)*, a contrast of the Chinese and the Tartars *(L'Orphelin de la Chine)*. In these works, as Voltaire would believe, the mores, which we know only on the stage, have been joined to passions which are often treated by the tragedian. Voltaire also advocates, at least for his own purpose, the use of characters from both high and low estates and the mingling of the mores of the country with those of the court. Subjects concerning these simple people can, therefore, be as proper to tragedy as the adventures of heroes who are well known (VI, 266-268).

The dramatic criticism of the last twenty years of Voltaire's career includes some very definite statements concerning the moral aim of tragedy. This had occupied his thoughts as early as 1743, when he had presented *Mahomet;* but in this final period, he demonstrates, both in theory and practice, that tragedy has a certain didactic purpose. In the dedication to the *Orphelin de la Chine*, Voltaire declares that the depiction of mores is nothing more than frivolous amusement unless it inspires virtue (V, 299).

The dedication of *Tancrède* (1760) professes a belief that the theater, where the taste of the youth is formed, is "une école toujours subsistante de poésie et de vertu." (V, 496). In a note accompanying *Olympie* (1764), Voltaire states that the public theater must be "l'école des moeurs" (VI, 127). Finally in the *discours* preceding *Les Guèbres* (1769), he reveals that the purpose of this play is to inspire "la charité universelle, le respect pour les lois, l'obéissance des sujets aux souverains, l'équité et l'indulgence des souverains pour leurs sujets." The object and final result of the play are to be "la morale la plus pure et la félicité publique" (VI, 491).

There are four miscellaneous articles of criticism to be considered in this final section. The first of these, the *Appel à toutes les nations* (1761), evidences a reaction against Shakespeare as well as against the English nation, which sees no real need to write tragedy guided by rules (XXIV, 203). Voltaire gives a brief historical sketch of the French theater with final remarks which point out the weaknesses of its drama. He agrees with Saint-Evremond that French plays do not make a strong enough impression, that in French tragedy, pity, emotion, and horror are replaced by *tendresse*, shock, and simple astonishment. In brief, Voltaire finds that there is a certain degree of warmth missing. He attributes the lassitude and weakness of the French to the construction of the theaters, to the shabbiness of its spectacle, and to the declamation of the actors (which he does indicate has been improved in recent years). The *Appel* ends, however, on a note of caution; for by wishing to perfect tragedy, one may possibly cause its ruination (XXIV, 218-221).

Voltaire's *Dictionnaire philosophique* contains an article entitled "Art Dramatique" were we find very brief discourses on the Italian, Spanish, and English theaters. In the latter section, Shakespeare is pronounced a genius by Voltaire, but almost in the same breath ranked below Harlequin, since men of letters in other countries take him to be "le plus misérable bouffon qui ait jamais amusé la populace" (XVII, 402). French tragedy is the next topic of discussion, and it is "la bonne tragédie française." Among the masterpieces, Voltaire gives preference to those tragedies which speak to the heart, rather than to those which speak only to the mind (XVII, 406).

The *Commentaire sur Corneille* (1764), if not the most important critical work of Voltaire, is certainly the most sustained. It contains analyses of the plays beginning with the *Médée*. There are added remarks on the three *discours* of Corneille, a playwright Voltaire tends to rank below Racine. The work contains attacks on such features as *galanterie*, long conversations, useless monologues, commonplaces and maxims, and the vain amusement of spectacle. The critic of the *Commentaire* remains in accord with established principles, for example, by pointing out the necessity for five acts, by extolling the merit of tragedy in verse, and by upholding the need for the liaison of scenes.

One of the most interesting aspects of the work is its views on catharsis, *vraisemblance,* and the unities. Voltaire frankly admits that he does not understand "this medecine" which is called the purgation of the passions. He does not understand how, according to Aristotle, pity and fear purge. What he does comprehend is the fact that while one is in the theater, he is agitated by the feeling of pity and fear. If he is a cultivated person, then he will sense a noble and delicate pleasure (XXXII, 349). Voltaire's further interpretation of catharsis is applied to the actor, who must create pity and fear if he is to be interesting. All other theories are considered vain and trifling by our critic (XXXII, 356).

Vraisemblance in tragic subjects is still regarded as necessary by Voltaire. The marvelous is made for opera, but "la tragédie est le pays de l'histoire, ou du moins de tout ce qui ressemble à l'histoire par la vraisemblance des faits et par la vérité des moeurs" (XXXII, 348). In a later passage, he gives his interpretation of Aristotle's statement that the poet is not to relate what has happened, but rather what has happened according to the law of probability or necessity:

> Choisissez la manière la plus vraisemblable, pourvu qu'elle soit tragique et non révoltante; et, si vous ne pouvez concilier ces deux choses, choisissez la manière dont la catastrophe doit arriver nécessairement par tout ce qui aura été annoncé dans les premiers actes (XXXII, 362).

In the *Commentaire,* Voltaire remains faithful to the unities, attributing all three to Aristotle (XXXII, 369). He regards an attack against them, particularly La Motte's, as a great heresy in literature (XXXII, 347). As for the unity of action, he does not recognize that a tragedy can have subordinate plots and diverse interests; a single action, however, without any episode, is regarded by Voltaire as perfection in art (XXXII, 364). The unity of time should be considered not only as a precept of Aristotle, but as a rule of nature. It would be more suitable for the action of a tragedy to last no longer than the presentation itself. This last statement is a repetition of what he had said as early as 1730 in the preface to *Oedipe;* but Voltaire's idea of the unity of place, here in the *Commentaire,* receives some modification and qualification. This unity is now considered to be almost impractical by the critic because of the poor construction of French theaters:

> Il faudrait que le théâtre fît voir aux yeux tous les endroits particuliers où la scène se passe, sans nuire à l'unité de lieu; ici une partie d'un temple, là le vestibule d'un palais, une place publique, des rues dans l'enfoncement... L'unité de lieu est tout le spectacle que l'œil peut embrasser sans peine (XXXII, 366-367).

The 1776 *Lettre à l'Académie Française* presents Voltaire's revolt against the *anglomanie* of the century and his final disparagement of Shakespeare. Racine is pitted against the English playwright to show that Voltaire prefers simplicity of exposition, the purity of diction of such a play as *Bajazet* instead of the useless material we see at the beginning of *Romeo and Juliet* (XXX, 359). He prefers a tragedian who will observe the unities, who will refuse to portray base characters or lofty ones who speak like "crocheteurs" (XXX, 354; 357). In short, Voltaire's plea to the Academy is an exhortation for the French to remain faithful to the ideals of Corneille, Racine, and Molière (XXX, 369).

In this last period of critical utterance, Voltaire calls attention to the fact that the French have distinguished themselves in tragedy and shown themselves to be superior in several ways to the dramatic poets of Athens (V, 496). Now he would have the tragic genre take on new life after his demise, acquiring beauties that he has not known, and purging itself of certain defects (VII, 171). These he does not name, but his final critical documents do restate principles and ideals on which he has already discoursed, principles which form a large part of the core of his doctrine: the affirmation that the theater should present love which is truly tragic, the conviction that tragedy is something other than a long conversation, the belief that beautiful and natural poetry can be linked to spectacle and display to achieve the artistic. He warns against the use of gigantic ideas lacking sense; never should the bizarre stand in the place of *nature* (IV, 269). The art of tragedy, with its annoying requirements such as rhyme, is still a noble one. Despite critical adventures and wanderings of some sixty years, Voltaire emerges as the champion of perfection in a dynamic theater where "il faut frapper l'âme et les yeux à la fois." He remains essentially a neo-classicist. [11]

---

[11] For discussion of this point, see Henry C. Lancaster, *French Tragedy in the Time of Louis XV and Voltaire* (1715-1774) (Baltimore: The Johns Hopkins Press, 1950), II, 610-613.

CHAPTER III

THE ABBÉ BATTEUX

The Abbé Charles Batteux (1713-1780), honorary Canon of Rheims, Professor of humanities at the Collège de Lisieux, of rhetoric at the College de Navarre, of philosophy, Greek, and Latin at the Collège de France, and member of the Académie Française,[1] attained some degree of renown as a theorist in his day through his treatise, *Les Beaux-Arts réduits à un même principe* (1746). This work and more importantly his *Cours de belles lettres*, first published in 1747, but bearing the title and subtitle *Principes de la littérature* in subsequent editions,[2] present the substance of Batteux's theory and view of tragedy.

As a foundation for the *Beaux-Arts*, Batteux presents the idea that there is a liaison and a fraternity which unites all the arts.[3] He does not wish to multiply the number of rules which exist; rather he would have us know that all rules are branches of the same system, that the imitation of nature is the common object of all the arts (pp. i-ii). They differ only through the means they use to execute this imitation (pp. ix-x). As imitations, the arts are only "*ressemblances*," employing the *vraisemblable* instead of the *vrai* (p. 14). We learn that the common link between Homer, Virgil, Terence, Raphael, Corneille, Le Brun, and Racine is their depiction

---

[1] Charles Collé, *Journal historique (1761-1762)*, ed. Bever, Boissy (Paris: Mercure de France, 1911), n., p. 76.

[2] *Catalogue général des livres imprimés dans la Bibliothèque Nationale* (Paris, 1901), VIII, 753-754.

[3] Charles Batteux, *Les Beaux-Arts réduits à un même principe* (Paris: Chez Durand, 1747), p. x. The citations from the *Beaux-Arts* which appear in parentheses refer to this edition.

of nature. Some of the above artists have used it with force and grace; others in this group have combined these two elements, but all of them have had the same object in mind "qui étoit de montrer des choses parfaites en elles-mêmes et en même temps intéressantes pour les hommes à qui ils devroient les montrer" (p. 91).

Chapter five of the *Beaux-Arts* is devoted to a consideration of tragedy which Batteux neatly divides into two types: the heroic and the marvelous. This latter form is in reality the opera or a "spectacle lyrique," as he calls it. Here the gods act as gods, employing supernatural power; but their operations go beyond the laws of *vraisemblance*. Heroic tagedy, or the real tragic genre as we think of it, is unveeringly linked to what is called the *naturel*. "C'est une représentation de grands hommes, une peinture, un tableau." Its merit consists of its resemblance to "le vrai" (pp. 218-222).

To this idea of the *vrai* is added Batteux's conception of the unmasking of art. For example, when one violates the unity of place or the unity of time, the spectator recognizes the artifice of the playwright. The former has seen the play begin and end in three hours and has also remained in the same spot while the scene has shifted. The imitation, thereby, becomes false. Useless episodes, inconsistent characters, epic descriptions, unconvincing actors — these will disrupt the harmony of the work and reveal that nature is acting simply to be acting (pp. 222-223).

Poetry, which for Batteux includes of course dramatic poetry, has for its aim pleasure, which is achieved by stirring the passions, by enlivening those which are not enemies of "sagesse." He further explains the passions to which he has reference:

> L'horreur du crime, à la suite duquel marchent la honte, la crainte, le repentir, sans compter les autres supplices: la compassion pour les malheureux, qui a presque une utilité aussi étendue que l'humanité même: l'admiration des grands exemples, qui laissent dans le cœur l'aiguillon de la vertu: un amour héroïque, et par conséquent légitime... (p. 157)

Poetry is not made to excite corruption in the hearts of men; it is to be the delight of virtuous souls. It is, moreover, not the pleasure of an indifferent art, but a satisfaction given the human heart which will not accept the mediocre, which will accept only such elements as extraordinary passions, great characters, and simple, natural denouement (p. 226).

The *Principes de la littérature,* augmented in various editions during the course of his lifetime, developed into a synthesis of Batteux's artistic ideals and precepts of literature; it therefore reveals a more complete attitude toward tragedy than is found in the *Beaux-Arts.* He begins by considering dramatic poetry in general. It incorporates an action which is a spectacle of the soul, where, unlike the gladiatorial combats, there is a humanizing effect, a gentle reaction, and infinite art, "puisque tout y est mensonge et qu'on veut le faire passer pour vérité." The persuasion of the dramatic poet who would have us accept his fiction as a reality must be supported by *vraisemblance* (based on the judgement of the eyes), the unities, the *récit,* proper decoration, and suitable declamation. The dramatist is never obliged, however, to treat things "dans la vérité historique." What Batteux calls "the truth of supposition" is as possible in dramatic composition as what he terms the real truth. It is most often necessary to add to a subject what it lacks and to remove from it what superfluous elements it contains. [4]

As for the question of *vraisemblance,* Batteux cites Aristotle's statement concerning this principle and proceeds to give his own interpretation. That which could happen is called "le possible," and that which should have occurred "le vraisemblable." The possible asks that nothing oppose the idea that the action was accomplished, while *vraisemblance* requires that there be some reason for the action to take place rather than not to occur. Batteux continues his explanation by dividing the possible into "le possible vraisemblable" and "le possible nécessaire." The multiplicity of events in the *Cid* can be explained by the former; the insult of Don Diègue and the ensuing vengeance by the latter (III, 10-12).

---

[4] Charles Batteux, *Principes de la littérature* (3 vols.; Paris: Desaint et Saillant, 1775), III, 5-10. Subsequent references to the *Principes* refer to this edition.

Batteux's idea of the dramatic, which he terms "le drame," possesses three sorts of unities: unity of action, unity of place, and "unité de jour." There is unity of action in a work when "on se propose un seul but, auquel tendent tous les moyens qu'on emploie." A tragedy can contain one or sometimes two actions, but they must be directed towards a common goal. When these actions are all on the same direct line, the action is simple and without episodes. If there are collateral actions only superficially attached to the principal action, then they are called episodic. The love of the Infanta for Rodrigue in the *Cid* is described as a violation of the rules because it fits nowhere in the main action; whereas, the love of Aricie for Hippolyte in *Phèdre* is linked to the action of the fourth act (III, 20-22).

The unity of time or "l'unité de jour" is, according to Batteux, "le tour de soleil ou vingt-quatre heures." This much, of course, the critic has taken from Aristotle; but he continues by saying that the action presented must begin and be completed in that space of time. It is rare, says Batteux, to find subjects which can be restricted to two or three hours, that is, the time required for their presentation. He therefore advises placing an entire night in the entr'acte and cleverly enough assigns the remaining excessive time to the three other *entr'actes*. He believes that a precise proportion is not necessary, since a half-hour on the stage could very well represent an hour: fifteen minutes, for example, could never stand for the length of a day (III, 27-28).

For Batteux the same indulgence, which broadens the limits of time, cannot extend the boundaries of place. The eye is not deceived, for if the place is changed without a change in décor, the spectator will be confused. If there is new scenery, then the charm of the illusion is broken. In nature, he reminds us, when the scene changes, we change place also. Batteux notes that the unity of place causes a great deal of torment and constraint for the dramatist. Corneille had great difficulty observing this rule in *Cinna*, where we see Auguste appearing in Emilie's *cabinet* to grant Cinna's pardon. This dramatist was of the opinion, recalls Batteux, that the place of action is not to be too distinctly marked; one can simply say that the scene is in Athens or Rome, or at least in one general location or another. The imagination of the spectator can fix a more specific locale if he really feels the need to do so (III, 29-31).

Before discussing the tragedy in more detail, Batteux adds to his treatise some suggestions for the dramatist. Sententious and moral thoughts, for example, should be avoided, as well as oratorical figures of speech; that is, if they cause repetition or unmask the conscious work of the artist. A monologue should be brief when used; when it is deemed necessary to write a long one, it should be the speech of an actor who is in a state of violent agitation. The *confident* has been invented, says Batteux, to avoid long and frequent monologues, but the role of these characters is ordinarily "si froid, que le remède ne vaut guères mieux que le mal" (III, 32-34).

Batteux defines tragedy as "la représentation d'une action héroïque, propre à exciter la terreur et la pitié" (III, 49). Theatrical action is composed of the conflict of interests and consequently a clash of the passions. Tragedy, more precisely, presents a violent conflict because it is concerned with the greatest interests, the extraordinary feats of heroes, the strength and might of men superior to other men (III, 51-52).

It is this idea of the heroic that Batteux pursues. It is a quality which accompanies the extraordinary. An action is heroic, for example, when it has a great operation to accomplish, such as the punishment of a tyrant or the acquiring of a throne (III, 53). One can quite possibly find touching events in the everyday life of the bourgeois, events which can be the object of poetic imitation; however, "s'il est vrai qu'on ne peut donner le brodequin aux rois, il n'est pas moins vrai qu'on ne peut ajuster le cothurne au marchand. La tragédie ne peut consentir à cette espèce de dégradation." The object of the arts is to aim always at the greatest, at that which is the noblest. The idea of the perfect *tragique* is found in subjects presenting kings, whose fall has more shock and produces a more shattering effect than it would have in the case of a middle class citizen (III, 54).

The pity and terror, which Batteux includes as elements in his definition of tragedy, and which he undoubtedly took from Aristotle, are further explored. Pity is aroused in us through viewing man in combat with his passions, weaknesses, and misfortunes. We are touched and moved because we see "notre semblable malheureux." Terror binds up our hearts because we fear for ourselves the misfortune we see in the lives of others. This fear, however, is alleviated by a certain gentleness when we make a secret comparison of our well being with the state of the unfortunate character who is suffering (III, 56). The stamp of tragedy is not the type of feeling it contains, but rather the kind it produces. Any tragedy which does not produce either pity or fear ("terreur," our critic calls it), is imperfect. If either one or the other is lacking, the play might only be "un spectacle héroïque" and not true tragedy (III, 58-59).

For Batteux there are three types of tragic heroes: the man who is entirely good (such as Polyeucte), the one who is entirely wicked (Atreus, for example), and the hero who stands in the middle path between the two (Oedipus). The virtuous man should continue to be so; the wicked should not cease to have an understanding which is evil; and the one following the mean between the two should be accompanied or preceded by an element which makes him subject to blame, for if this said action is neither good nor bad in itself, then the hero has no character. If the action were only partially wicked, the tragic character would lack the necessary heroic quality. The veritable "tragique" therefore, is the virtuous man — at least more virtuous than evil — who is the victim of his duty (such as Curiace), or of his own weakness (Phèdre), or victim of another man (Polyeucte). Oedipus also is a suitable hero, since he becomes the victim of fatality. It is here that Batteux relies on Aristotle's recommendation for the portrayal of the tragic hero (III, 59-60).

Terror is distinguished from horror in Batteux's terminology by citing the example of Thyestes drinking the blood of his son. This is "horreur" and not "terreur." There is no necessity for the spilling of blood in order to arouse tragic feeling: Ariadne abandoned on the isle of Naxos, Philoctetes alone in his cave on the isle of Lemos — these are tragic situations because they are as cruel as death itself. These are situations where one sees intertwined grief, despair, and dejection (III, 66).

In the *Beaux-Arts* Batteux had spoken of the great examples which tragedy firnishes, and how they become the goad or incentive for virtue. Now, in the *Principes,* he makes more concise statements regarding the moral aim of tragedy. He denies that this genre is a lesson or an instruction, for a didactic concept would deny tragedy its real object. Virtue rewarded excites only joy, not terror and pity. He would agree with Corneille, who, in the dedication to *Médée*, states that dramatic poetry describes for us, in an indifferent fashion, good and evil actions without proposing that we accept the latter as examples of conduct (III, 68-69).

Batteux's statement that tragedy is "un exercice de l'âme par des émotions tristes" (III, 70), leads to his interpretation of Aristotelian catharsis. He believes that this element refers to pity and terror which are purified, "c'est-à-dire, leur ôter ce qu'elles peuvent avoir ou de trop ou d'étranger, qui les empêcheroit d'être aussi profitables qu'elles le seroient sans cela." Thus, pity and fear, when purified or purged, can become useful. Their purgation is a sort of refinement which makes them useful for humanity. In their purified state, they can help one to bear his burdens more easily; the spectator will be able to look on his own misfortunes, judging and measuring them with his courage (III, 75-77).

Batteux is an example of a neo-classic critic, a spiritual descendant of Boileau, decreeing laws and precepts from his Parnassian seat.[5] He is a critic whose theories emerge as interpretations of Aristotle, an attestation of the orthodoxy of the *Poetics*. Not only does Batteux accept the Greek philosopher as a guide to the understanding and meaning of tragedy, but he also professes belief in "le grand Corneille," who dispelled the clouds and cleaned the horizon of the French theater (III, 111). Through his doctrine, Batteux renders account of the high calling of the dramatic poet, the certain demands of his art (III, 77-79). From this point of view, he deserves the momentary fame, the fleeting enjoyment of having an audience,[6] who accepted him as the spokesmen for an age of reason.

---

[5] See Saintsbury's classification of Batteux as a critic. *A History of Criticism* (3 vols.; New York: Dood Mead and Co., 1902), II, 522-525.

[6] Voltaire speaks of Batteux's talent with derision: *Œuvres complètes* (Paris: Garnier, 1881), XLI, 262; Grimm, however, has faint praise for him in the *Correspondance littéraire* (Paris: Garnier, 1878), III, 510. The Abbé Raynal tells of the success of the *Beaux-Arts* and says that it is well written: *Correspondance littéraire*, I, 127.

CHAPTER IV

GRIMM AND HIS VIEW OF TRAGEDY IN THE
CORRESPONDANCE LITTÉRAIRE

Frédéric-Melchior Grimm (1723-1807) exerted a certain influence and enjoyed some renown in the eighteenth century, but since we today know him only through the *Correspondance littéraire,* which was kept secret during his lifetime and only partially edited in 1812, his celebrity has been for the most part posthumous.[1] Why Grimm suddenly decided to leave Leipzig and come to Paris in 1749 is not known.[2] We do know from Rousseau's *Confessions* that while waiting for better employment in the French capital, he served as *lecteur* to the Prince of Saxe-Gotha and later as secretary to the Count of Friesen.[3] Grimm drafted the first issue of the *Correspondance* in May of 1753, and except for rare exceptions, he sent every two weeks letters of varying length to the subscribers,[4] who included Catherine the Great, the King of Poland, and the Queen of Sweden.[5] The enterprise ceased in March of 1773, when Grimm definitely gave over his work to Meister.[6]

---

[1] André Cazes, *Grimm et les Encyclopédistes* (Paris: Les Presses Universitaires, 1933), p. 5.
[2] Anne Cutting Jones, *Frederick-Melchior Grimm As a Critic of Eighteenth-Century Drama* (Bryn Mawr: Bryn Mawr College, 1926), p. 24.
[3] Cazes, p. 10.
[4] *Ibid.*, p. 36.
[5] René Wellek, *A History of Modern Criticism: 1750-1950* (4 vols.; New Haven: Yale University Press, 1955), II, 71.
[6] Cazes, p. 37.

The idea of a *correspondance littéraire* was not original with Grimm. Others such as La Harpe (writing for the Grand Duke of Russia) and Raynal (for the Duchess of Saxe-Gotha) had reported events taking place in Paris. Grimm's journal is interesting because it faithfully records the literary activity of the important years of the last half of the century — and with more thoroughness than the other efforts at evaluating the belles-lettres of the era.[7] In the preface to his *Correspondance,* Grimm made it quite clear that a large part of his reviews would be devoted to drama.[8] As a student at the University of Leipzig, he had published a tragedy, which reveals his familiarity with classic and French models.[9] Now he was prepared, by examining the dramatic material available, to make the foreign reader in particular aware of trends and ideas in the French literary world.[10]

One of Grimm's prevailing attitudes in the *Correspondance littéraire* is his lament for the present state of French tragedy, which he relates to and continually associates with the past masters of the genre. To this general theme, he adds a plea for genius, which in turn evokes the memory of a bygone excellence. The public, he says, prefers ballets and pantomime to the masterpieces of Corneille, and this is humiliating for French taste. He actually speaks of the Comédie-Française as being in a state of decadence, devoid of successors who can uphold the quality found in Corneille and Racine.[11] The genius which produced Corneille's work is indispensable in the arts (III, 498); it is not subjects which are lacking to the French theater, but men of genius, who still have open before them a multitude of treasures (IV, 182). These subjects are never exhausted for the superior man, since the merit of a great work of art depends on how it is treated (IX, 26).

---

[7] Jones, p. 3.
[8] *Ibid.,* p. 9.
[9] *Ibid.,* p. 20. The name of the tragedy was *Banise,* published in 1743. See: Billy, *Diderot* (Paris: Les Editions de France, 1932), p. 151.
[10] Jones, p. 3.
[11] Frédéric-Melchior Grimm, *Correspondance littéraire,* ed. Maurice Tourneux (16 vols.; Paris: Garnier, 1877-82), II, 263. Subsequent citations in parentheses refer to this edition.

Not only does Grimm revere the tragedians of the seventeenth century, but he clearly evidences his esteem for the Greek tragic playwrights. He praises, for example, Sophocles' *Philoctetes* for its simplicity, its majestic naiveté, and for its sublimity (II, 504). He asks if there is a nation which has a tragedy to compare with this masterpiece. It is a bitter and cruel criticism of French taste to observe that this play would be presented without success in the French theater; whereas, among the spectators of Athens, terrible effects — instead of sterile tears — would be produced (III, 377). Greek tragedies did not fear to present terrifying actions. It is simply a question of being able to stage a scene with enough truth to produce the terrible impressions which should result from it (III, 407). When Grimm discusses Quinault's *Alceste,* he summons up the memory of the Euripides play and again uses the adjective sublime in speaking of an ancient tragedy (III, 465). Later in the *Correspondance,* he returns to the idea of simplicity among the ancients and adds that the French are "bien loin de ce grand goût des anciens, qui sera éternellement le modèle pour juger tout ce qui est beau dans les arts et dans la nature" (IV, 37). This simplicity will remain "la loi et le modèle du beau" (IV, 89). To imitate the ancients, however, is not to copy their works; it is to create by their examples, using genius which knows how to find the characteristics and harmony of each element. A poet copying the sublime tragedies of the Athenian theater will not obtain a place beside Sophocles and Euripides by so doing. The modern playwright must invent situations, scenes, and *discours* which are sublime, true, *pathétiques,* and powerful enough to support their comparison to ancient tragedy (VI, 95). On two occasions Grimm speaks of the restricted area of the French stage which has not been utilized to its fullest. Domestic events, not suited to the immensity of the Greek theater, for example, could be offered to the public, who would receive as great an impression as by seeing gods and heroes played by actors with "une taille défectueuse" (IV, 461).

In a section of the *Correspondance* entitled "Réflexions sur la Tragédie," Grimm again draws a comparison between ancient and modern tragedy. For the ancients, this genre was a political institution, an act of religion; for the French, on the other hand, it is a matter of amusement. In Greece and Rome, the people attended the spectacle in a body, and by doing so, satisfied a duty. Tragedy in France, having become a pastime, could therefore not conserve its dignity and importance as a public and religious institution. If the Greeks and Romans could see the tragedies which the French regard as great, they would judge them to be child's play. The ancients would show more maturity because of their political and educational background. In ancient Greece, the dramatist was not only a poet, but a statesman who composed tragedies for the instruction of the people. At this point, Grimm launches into a tirade against modern tragedy, calling it a system of convention and *fantaisie,* denatured and false. Naturalness, truth, and simplicity have absolutely disappeared (VI, 170-172).

Grimm's attention is directed not only to the Greek theater, but also to the English stage, and more particularly to a consideration of Shakespeare. In speaking of Voltaire's *Appel à toutes les nations,* he censures the author for forgetting the debt he owes the English theater. Voltaire, says Grimm, took more from the English than from the ancients, whom he knew about only from what he learned as a student (IV, 341). Later Grimm refers to the irregularity of Shakespeare, but adds that a play like *Henry VI* depicts mores which are stronger and truer, for example, than those found in La Harpe's *Warrick,* a play treating the same subject (V, 417). Racine's lines charm the ear, but they do not represent the real accent of nature. What Grimm avows he is looking for is that quality of being less beautiful, less arranged, and instead more savage, more sublime. This he finds in Shakespeare's finest work, but seeks in vain among the creations of French tragic poets (VI, 173). Grimm ultimately hands down a defense of the Bard with the following statement: "Quoi qu'on fasse et quoi qu'on écrive, il faudra toujours reconnaître dans Shakespeare un homme d'un grand et sublime génie" (VI, 321).

A number of specific abuses practiced by writers of French tragedy occupy Grimm's thoughts in the *Correspondance.* He attacks first of all "maximes communes et usées," which he says are disfiguring modern tragedies (II, 382). These maxims and commonplaces appear at moments when there should be no moralization, or else they are used as allusions to political situations, thereby revealing the attempt of the author to win acclamation and admiration (III, 158-159). The only sententious statement appropriate for use in tragic dialogue is the one induced by passion and the strength of dramatic situation (IV, 362).

Grimm also attacks the prevailing use in tragedy of an insipid type of love, which, he considers, had already become an essential element in French tragedy by the time Voltaire began to write for the theater. Grimm reproaches Racine for his use of love — "cette passion puérile et subalterne." It was he who spoiled the subject of *Phèdre*, by including the Aricie episode; *Iphigénie*, by presenting Eriphile in love; and *Andromaque*, by depicting an amorous Hermione (V, 385). Among other things, he censures Corneille for transforming love and passion into reasoning and commonplace, instead of depicting it in terms of the most secret movements of the soul (V, 503).

French tragedies, in the eyes of Grimm, are too full of *discours* (V, 462). Along with commonplaces and maxims, he lambastes false *discours* (VI, 18), the affected ones which lack tragic force (IV, 437). He finds, moreover, that French dramatic poets have abused the use of dreams in their plays, and this has become a childish device. Grimm implies, through one statement, that he favors action over the *récit* (II, 397); in another, that there is no real necessity for five acts, since in a single one the poet who could include the movements of terror and compassion would demonstrate as much genius as the person who chooses to make his tragedy "un recueil de beaux vers en cinq cahiers" (III, 84). He also attacks the multiplicity of events in a tragedy and claims that this factor shows a defect in *invention* and stands contrary to *vérité* (V, 15; 158). He recalls that the unity of action was, above all, respected by the ancients; in French plays, however,

> il arrive ordinairement plus d'incidents durant l'espace de quelques heures qu'il n'en arrive dans la réalité pendant une longue suite d'années: on peut dire que nos héros sont, au premier acte, à cent lieues de la catastrophe qui les attend au cinquième. Cela donne à nos drames un vernis de faux qui en empêche l'effet, aussi au bout d'un quart d'heure l'impression la plus forte est effacée (V, 157).

The more physical aspects of tragedy are criticized by citations which profess Grimm's belief in more realistic costuming and show his desire for more natural declamation in tragedy (III, 89; 157-158).

By far the most striking reform advocated by Grimm concerns the question of prose versus verse. He offers more specific remarks and comments regarding this controversy than for any other single problem he approaches. Near the beginning of the *Correspondance* (in March of 1755), he recommends that a play such as Sophocles' *Philoctetes,* if treated by a modern tragedian, be translated (he no doubt means adapted) to conserve its original simplicity, and be presented in prose, "parce que nos vers sont trop maniérés pour ne point tuer un sujet aussi grave que celui-là" (II, 504). In October of 1760, when reviewing Voltaire's *Tancrède,* Grimm recalls how the *vers croisés* of this play disconcerted the *parterre.* He admits that the use of this innovation produces less monotony, but feels that Voltaire should have gone even further and composed his tragedy in *vers libres,* that is, not only *croisés,* but of varying length. This would tend to make the *discours* closer to prose and at the same time move them further from tedium (IV, 293). In April of 1764, Grimm again discusses the question of verse in the theater; and again he thinks of the problem, at least in part, from the standpoint of the ancients and their simplicity:

> ... le vers français sera toujours un langage trop apprêté, trop arrondi pour convenir à la poésie dramatique. C'est lui, n'en doutons point, qui a éloigné le théâtre français de cette simplicité, de ce naturel, de cette énergie concise et sublime qui font le prix du théâtre ancien et le charme des gens de goût (V, 477-478).

Verse has been responsible for the epic deviations, the tirades which are so contrary to the idea of theatrical *bienséance.* Rhyme also, according to Grimm, tends to divert the author from his subject, suggesting to him *discours* which should not be written. He informs the reader that the ancients used iambic meter for dramatic discourse, and that this form possessed none of the "inconvénients de nos vers alexandrins." In short, the alexandrine is monotonous and unsuitable for theatrical declamation (V, 478). In January of 1765, Grimm mentions the alexandrine again, ascribing to it the adjectives monotonous and false. It has deprived

French tragedy of its naturalness (VI, 173-174). In September of 1767, there is another attack on the alexandrine, and this time it is criticized for being incompatible with truth and naturalness in dialogue. The merit of writing in verse has an additional merit if the lines can retain simplicity, conciseness, and naturalness so far as dialogue is concerned. But French verse, Grimm remarks, does not observe prosody in its verse; it counts syllables without attention to their meter, and thereby the language stands little chance of ever having what he considers a true dramatic verse (VII, 415-416). Grimm advocates, as late as February of 1770, that tragedy be written in prose, since the French, unlike the Greeks, Romans, and modern Italians, do not have a dramatic verse. A Dido, placed on the stage, cannot speak the divine language of Virgil; for, if so, the play becomes epic and not dramatic poetry (VIII, 460).

In discussing Crébillon's *Triumvirat*, Grimm reproaches French authors for having too greatly "francisé" the subjects from antiquity and from foreign sources. This is especially unbearable in the treatment of Roman events, because, says Grimm, we are more familiar with their history than with that of any other nation. Corneille did not have the Romans speak as true Romans, and this is called by our critic "un défaut de bienséance nationale." This principle also involves a "défaut de mœurs" (II, 361). Later in the *Correspondance*, he speaks of a falseness which reigns in French tragedy: "La peinture des mœurs étrangères est sans doute précieuse; mais pourquoi y employer des couleurs françaises?" He would prefer not to see these Romans, Greeks, Persians and Scythians on the stage, if they are to speak French ideas (VII, 209). This does not mean that he frowns on the use of historical subjects; for, in fact, he finds that invented subjects almost always lack color and strength so far as details are concerned (VII, 399).

In April of 1754, Grimm included in the midst of his reviews a definite statement regarding the didactic and moral purpose of the theater. He remarks that if every painting which presents virtue unrewarded is dangerous, then we should have to proscribe painting and all the fine arts, as well as the study of history; we should, moreover, have to cease living with our fellow man. It is quite common to see virtue become the victim of vice or crime. Plays, therefore, should depict for us men as they actually are, with their passions, virtues, and vices. The real merit of the presentation is enclosed in the question of whether "le tableau est vrai, bien choisi, bien fait." If these qualities exist, the work is to be regarded as good and beyond reproach. The merit of the drama is not one of edification; rather it is made to enlighten us, to form our taste, and to make us sensitive beings. The Romans, continues Grimm, presented gladiatorial combats to familiarize the populace with the horrors of war; but the principal advantage of French tragedy can be the salutary, compassionate effect it has on the people, and there can be no surer means to this end than to give frequent occasions for the shedding of tears (II, 335). Much later in the *Correspondance* (July, 1764), Grimm seems to reverse his position with regard to the moral purpose of the theater. Here he would like to see the theater become "une école publique de mœurs" rather than a place of amusement for a certain group of citizens (VI, 34).

The allusion to theoretical principles of two other critics, Hume and Marmontel, concerning tragedy, provokes on the part of Grimm reflexion and conjecture with regard to the genre. Hume's theory of tragedy, as presented in the *Correspondance*, states that the pleasure we receive from a tragic scene is due to the genius of the poet, to his eloquence, and to his art; in fact, to the assembly of so many talents, which win our admiration and divert our more painful emotions. To this general theory Grimm adds the idea that the more the poet leaves for the imagination to consider, the more he will be sure of affecting it — and in a violent fashion. Pantomime and music move us with a hundred times more violence than poetry and painting, simply because the musician and the mime leave more of a task for the imagination than does the artist with his colors. A pathetic speech from the works of Sophocles or Euripides will leave with the spectator admiration for their genius, but the impression received will be less violent, less involuntary than the one caused by a clever pantomime (IV, 174). Thus we see that these ideas, written by Grimm in January of 1760, manifest his adhesion to the principles set forth in Diderot's *De la poésie dramatique*.

Marmontel's theory (found in the *Eléments de littérature*) relative to the essential difference between Greek tragedy and French tragedy incites Grimm to attack the ideas presented by the former.

Ancient tragedy, according to Marmontel, was completely based on the idea of fatality, while the interest of modern tragedy rests in the passions and their development. This variety of subject matter at the disposal of the moderns does not grant them the superiority that Marmontel would assign them. Both fatality and the passions "sont également fondées sur l'immuable nécessité qui décide du sort de l'homme." If passions and their deviations were free agents, there would be no pity, no interest in tragedy. The misfortunes which they produce would be able neither to frighten nor to move the spectator. No matter which passion one chooses to place on the stage, "elle ne peut intéresser qu'autant qu'elle dispose de votre personnage aussi aveuglément et aussi impérieusement que la fatalité dispose de ses vertus et de son bonheur" (V, 388).

Grimm is a severe critic of not only the tragedy of his era, but also of the public and its tastes. Even Racine and Corneille, the great models, are not without defects; but Grimm is most definitely pessimistic regarding the legacy his century will leave. What will posterity say, he demands, about these many tragedies in which *bon sens* and *vraisemblance* are constantly sacrificed; in which *mauvais goût* stifles *simplicité* and the *naturel;* in which the marvelous takes the place of the sublime? (V, 186). Grimm is obviously not a thorough classicist, for as an enemy of the alexandrine, an admirer of Shakespeare, and a supporter of Diderot, he points to new developments in French drama. Perhaps the most revealing question he asks is whether true tragedy has yet been found in France (VII, 416).

CHAPTER V

DIDEROT AND TRAGEDY

In 1757, while the battle over the *Encyclopédie* raged, the still-confident Denis Diderot published his play, *Le Fils naturel*. Other preoccupations were cast aside, for after all, the theater was supposedly his first love, his "démon." [1] While still very young, he had thought of being an actor; [2] and on leaving the Collège de Louis-le-Grand, for fifteen years he was an assiduous frequenter of Parisian theaters, including the Opéra. [3] There followed in 1758 his second *drame*, *Le Père de famille*, and although neither play was produced by the Comédie-Française before it was published — the *Père de famille* was presented in 1761 and the *Fils naturel* in 1771 — Diderot created a storm of interest in the capital.

If we cannot consider Diderot the first great practitioner of what he called the *genre sérieux*, we can at least view him as its greatest theorist. [4] His theories of drama were, indeed, the most influential of his critical writings of the time; and it has been observed that Diderot as a critic is known mostly by the critical documents accompanying the plays mentioned above — the *Entretiens sur le Fils naturel* and the *Discours sur la poésie*

---

[1] André Billy, *Diderot* (Paris: Les Editions de France, 1932), p. 212.
[2] Arthur M. Wilson, *Diderot: The Testing Years* (New York: Oxford University Press, 1957), p. 264.
[3] Yvon Belaval, *L'Esthétique sans paradoxe de Diderot* (Paris: Gallimard, 1950), p. 19.
[4] Wilson, pp. 260-261.

dramatique (something of an epilogue for the *Père de famille*). These works are not only manifestoes of the *drame bourgeois*, presenting ideas new in France,[5] but together with sentiments expressed in his novel, *Les Bijoux indiscrets* (1748), they become the critical expression of Diderot with regard to tragedy.[6]

Chapter 38 of the *Bijoux indiscrets* offers a critical discussion of drama with the following participants: Mangogul, sultan of a mythical Congo kingdom; Selim, his courtier; Ricaric, member of the *académie congeoise;* and Mirzoza, the favorite of the Sultan. Selim defends modern authors, opposing Ricaric, who is attached only to the ancient rules. The only requirement of the courtier is that he be pleased by a work; for him there is no other rule except the imitation of nature, Ricaric challenges this attitude by citing his belief that all the faces of nature are true, although not equally beautiful. Selim would like to know, at any rate, how it is, having surpassed the ancients in astronomy, navigation, physics, why then have the moderns not also been superior to them in matters of poetry. Mirzoza then speaks in defense of the ancients, calling modern tragedy inferior to that of the Greeks and Romans. These ancient peoples wrote natural, simple dialogue; their denouements were not forced, and their subjects were noble, simple, and free from a multiplicity of episodes. She mentions a play which we recognize as Sophocles' *Philoctetes*, praising it for its perfection, the same degree of which no modern play can claim. Selim agrees, stating that "nos pièces sont un peu chargées; mais c'est un mal nécessaire; sans le secours des épisodes, on se morfondrait." The conversation ends with Mirzoza's attack against the unnaturalness of dialogue, and there is a now famous reference to a French dramatist:

> L'emphase, l'esprit et le papillotage qui y règnent sont à mille lieues de la nature. C'est en vain que l'auteur cherche à se dérober; mes yeux percent, et je l'aperçois

---

[5] René Wellek, *A History of Modern Criticism: 1750-1950* (New Haven: Yale University Press, 1955), I, 47.

[6] Anne C. Jones cites the fact that Diderot became a regular editor of Grimm's *Correspondance littéraire* in 1759, but that by that date he had already formulated his dramatic theories. See: *Frederick-Melchior Grimm As a Critic of Eighteenth Century Drama* (Bryn Mawr: Bryn Mawr College, 1926), p. 60.

> sans cesse derrière ses personnages. Cinna, Sertorius, Maxime, Emilie sont à tout moment les sarbacanes de Corneille... [7]

She also reveals her scorn for the miraculous, poorly-handled denouement and censures contemporary declamation, costume, and acting. Even if a play is an imitation of an event and not the event itself, Mirzoza finds that the action can be presented in the most natural manner (IV, 283-287).

This section of the *Bijoux indiscrets* is a manifestation of Diderot's displeasure, almost a decade before the *Entretiens* accompanying the *Fils naturel* with the French theater. The references, although perhaps thinly veiled like others pertaining to politics and music in the novel,[8] give a clear indication that he did not share his compatriots' high idea of the state of drama in France (IV, 280n.). A more formal development of his theories and suggestions lies ahead.

Relative to tragedy, the first *entretien* with Dorval is concerned first of all with the unities. Dorval admits that these laws are difficult to observe, but they are, at the same time, "sensées." He prefers, for example, that a play be simple, rather than "chargée d'incidents." He says, moreover:

> L'art d'intriguer consiste à lier les événements de manière que le spectateur sensé y aperçoive toujours une raison qui le satisfasse. La raison doit être d'autant plus forte, que les événements sont plus singuliers (VII, 88).

According to Dorval, one cannot be too severe about the unity of place. Without this unity, what he terms the "conduite" of a play is always obstructed and hampered; it becomes equivocal and dubious. The discussion of this particular unity gives rise to a plea for a change of scenery — that is, if the place must forcibly change. This practice would cause the performance to become more varied, more interesting, and clearer for the spectator.

---

[7] Denis Diderot, *Œuvres complètes*, ed. Jules Assézat et Maurice Tourneux (20 vols.; Paris: Garnier, 1875-1877), IV, 285-286. Subsequent citations in parentheses refer to this specific edition.

[8] Wilson, p. 84.

Dorval finds that it is unreasonable, for example, to have courtiers conspire against their sovereign in the very place where he has come to consult them. He has, of course, *Cinna* in mind (VII, 88-89).

In the *premier entretien,* Diderot (as the interlocutor "Moi") differentiates between a *coup de théâtre* and the *tableau,* which will become so much an essential part of his *drame bourgeois.* The *coup de théâtre* is defined as "un incident imprévu qui se passe en action, et qui change subitement l'état des personnages." The *tableau* would involve the natural placement or arrangement of these characters on the stage, so if the scene were copied by a painter, it would be capable of pleasing. Dorval is of the opinion that a well-constructed and well-presented dramatic work would offer the spectator "autant de tableaux réels qu'il y aurait dans l'action de moments favorables au peintre" (VII, 95). The general conclusion of this section is that *coups de théâtre* are bad, and if used, should be relative to fact and not fiction (VII, 96-100).

The *second entretien* attacks the *discours,* and here the comments are very pertinent to tragedy. The true and great speeches, says Dorval, have as their source great interests and great passions. He also reminds his interlocutor that almost all men speak well in the act of dying. The French, however, speak too much in their drama; consequently, there is not enough action. Here the idea is also introduced that pantomime is very neglected in the modern theater; it is a lost art, which the ancients were able to utilize effectively. The important thing, especially in the spectacle of great passion, is the combination of the actor's voice, gestures, and actions (VII, 104-106).

Dorval speaks next of the tirade and defines it as "un ramage opposé à ces vraies voix de la passion." It may be well applauded, but nothing is in worst taste. As long as this practice continues, the action is suspended, and in reality the stage is left bare. The actor, by using this sort of speech, places himself out of his role; the author, too, has left behind his subject. Both have abandoned the stage and have descended into the *parterre* (VII, 106).

There is a plea on the part of Dorval for the use of more realistic stage setting and the execution of new tableaux (VII, 114). Here Diderot, the theorist, advances the idea of a theater "très-étendu," where, just as in nature, there would be concurrent actions, which would fortify each other to produce terrible effects. No more fleeting, small emotions; for now the spectator's soul will be besieged by trouble and fear, recalling the effect of ancient tragedy. This idea would be achieved, at least in part, by combining the pantomime with the *discours*, and by alternating "une scène parlée avec une scène muette" (VII, 115-116).

In the second *entretien*, Dorval advocates a "tragédie domestique et bourgeoise," which is to be written in prose. He recalls that Shakespeare's tragedies are half-verse, half-prose (VII, 120). Since the comedy has already made use of prose,[9] now tragedy can employ it to make us weep. The French have retained the pomposity of versification possessed by the ancients, but Dorval points out that this suited their spacious theaters, where, in a vast area, the passions could be communicated, even by the tears of one great person. This bombast was in accord, moreover, with their language of marked accent and with their declamation, which was accompanied by instruments. While conserving this characteristic of the ancients, the theater of France has abandoned "la simplicité de l'intrigue, et la vérité des tableaux" (VII, 121).

The third *entretien* attempts, through the eyes of Dorval, to establish a dramatic system, which is reduced to the following: "le burlesque, le genre comique, le genre sérieux, le genre tragique, le merveilleux." From this classification it is decided that the "genre comique" and the "genre tragique" are the real limits or boundaries of dramatic composition. It is possible to call burlesque to the aid of comedy without degrading it, and likewise to encroach upon the resources of the marvelous for tragic composition; but the comic and tragic genres, occupying the extremities, are considered by Diderot "les plus frappants et les plus difficiles." Because of this difficulty, the beginning playwright should try the *genre sérieux* before attempting to write a tragedy (VII, 135-136). He should remember that to a lesser degree, it is

---

[9] Through the ideas of the interlocutors in the *Paradoxe sur le comédien*, Diderot attacks French dramatic verse. The first speaker calls the alexandrine "trop nombreux et trop noble pour le dialogue." The second speaker pronounces the ten-syllable line as "trop futile et trop léger." *Œuvres complètes*, VIII, 406.

not the subject which makes a play a comedy, or a *drame sérieux,* or a tragedy; it is rather the tone, the passions, the characters, and the interest which mold the composition. The effects of love, jealousy, ambition, hate, and envy can make one laugh, think, or tremble (VII, 140).

Dorval advocates again, in this last dialogue, a *tragédie domestique,* calling it "le tableau des malheurs qui nous environnent," and thereby suggesting that it is a genre closer to us than the accepted tragedy. Let the playwright neglect *coups de théâtre,* it is again urged, in order to draw near to real life through the use of *tableaux* and pantomime (VII, 145-146). Almost as a matter of summary, Dorval sets forth the work of the present century, viewing it as a type of legacy from the century past, or as a definite responsibility: the *tragédie bourgeoise* must be created, and here the pantomime must be closely connected to the action; condition must be substituted for *caractère,* perhaps in all the genres; a real tragedy must be introduced to the lyric theater. This tragedy is the one which Dorval calls "ancienne," for the *tragédie domestique,* of course, excludes versification; and as explained, "la tragédie, et en général toute composition dramatique destinée pour la scène lyrique, doit être mesurée." Dorval cites, for example, certain lines from Racine's *Iphigénie,* [10] which he finds highly suitable for musical imitation. Clytemnestra's emotion can be presented by the musician "dans toutes ses nuances." She begins with a type of recitative, and then in the fourth line, the melody begins. The result becomes a symphony as lamentation, grief, fright, horror, and fury are depicted (VII, 162-163).

As in the third *entretien,* Diderot now establishes in his *De la poésie dramatique* a dramatic system. It includes this time the *comédie gaie,* whose object is to criticize and ridicule vice; the *comédie sérieuse,* which is destined to present an idea of virtue and the duties of man; *tragédie,* "qui aurait pour objet nos

---

[10] Act V, scene iv:
 ... O mère infortunée!
 De festons odieux ma fille couronnée,
 Tend la gorge aux couteaux par son père apprêtés.
 Calchas va dans son sang ... Barbares! arrêtez;
 C'est le pur sang du dieu qui lance le tonnerre...
 J'entends gronder la foudre et sens trembler la terre.
 Un dieu vengeur, un dieu fait retenir ces coups.

malheurs domestiques"; another type of tragedy, "qui a pour objet les catastrophes publiques et les malheurs des grands" (VII, 308-309). The didactic purposes of Diderot, the critic, are emphasized as he states that one must always have virtue and virtuous men in view when writing, that all the arts of imitation would aid mankind if only they could join in a common objective — the creation of a love for virtue and a detestation for vice. By going to the theater, men will save themselves from the company of the wicked, finding on the stage those with whom they would like to live, seeing humanity as it really exists, and in turn being reconciled with it. Diderot thus sees the theater as an organ of public instruction, since every nation has prejudices to destroy, vices to pursue, and ridicules to decry (VII, 310).

This *discours* accompanying the *Père de famille* speaks of the "conduite simple" of ancient drama, of its action "prise le plus près de sa fin." It is further characterized by energetic speeches, strong passions, *tableaux,* and the firm depiction of one or two characters (VII, 316). Modern playwrights, on the other hand, are criticized for their violation of the unity of action; for Diderot finds that it is almost impossible to maintain two plots at the same time. One will achieve interest at the expense of the other. The dramatic poet guilty of the disregard of this unity will then be faced with the necessity of resolving both plots at the same instant (VII, 317). There are other recommendations for the dramatist. He must first have a plan; and turning to Aristotle [11] for support of this idea, and applying it next to all types of drama, Diderot concludes that once the plan or outline has been made, one can consequently think of all the episodes which accompany it. As for interest, it is necessary to have one's characters in mind rather than the spectators. It is the characters who should advance towards the denouement without suspecting it. Interest demands many times that the spectator know clearly what will happen, and there is an advantage in seeing the genesis of the dramatic storm. The recognition scene between Zaïre and Nérestan, for example,

---

[11] Diderot calls Aristotle "un philosophe qui marche avec ordre, qui établit des principes généraux, et qui en laisse les conséquences à tirer, et les applications à faire." *Œuvres complètes,* VII, 322.

would have had greater impact if the spectator had been warned of it. Like the man of the *parterre*, Diderot feels no terror, being unaware that Nero is listening to the conversation between Britannicus and Junie. Often the title of a tragedy announces the denouement, simply because it is a fact to be found in history (VII 342-343).

Contrast of character is considered in Diderot's discourse, but chiefly in relation to the *drame*. He states his reason:

> Plus un genre sera sérieux, moins il ne semblera admettre le contraste. Il est rare dans la tragédie. Si on l'y introduit, ce n'est qu'entre les subalternes. Le héros est seul. Il n'y a point de contraste dans *Britannicus*, point dans *Andromaque*, point dans *Cinna*, point dans *Zaïre* (VII, 351).

Thus displeased by this element in tragedy, Diderot abandons it as a legacy for the farce, reminding the reader that the theorists have nothing to say about contrast in their poetics (VII, 351-354).

In speaking of dramatic dialogue, Diderot finds that no one has possessed this art to the same degree as Corneille:

> Ses personnages se pressent sans ménagements; ils parent et portent en même temps; c'est une lutte. La réponse ne s'accroche pas au dernier mot de l'interlocuteur; elle touche à la chose et au fond. Arrêtez-vous où vous voudrez; c'est toujours celui qui parle, qui vous paraît avoir raison (VII, 364).

This is close to what he had stated in the second *entretien*; it is almost a renewed cry for more natural dialogue, for dramatic speech which is naturally linked. Racine's dialogue, on the other hand, is characterized as "difficile," for the statements and the responses are linked only by such delicate sensations, such fleeting ideas, such rapid movements of the soul, that they appear to be loose and incoherent (VII, 364-365). Diderot concludes his section on dialogue with a statement which he labels as a general rule for the art of poetry, and for which there is no exception: "C'est que le monologue est un moment de repos pour l'action et de trouble pour le personnage" (VII, 368).

The *De la poésie dramatique* ends with a discussion of costume, scenery, and pantomime. This section is largely a protest against prevailing conditions which permit a falseness and poverty of decoration and reveals, so far as Diderot is concerned, that the French are still far from possessing good taste.[12] The unity of place is a rule which one is required to respect, but at the same time, the stage is given over to "un mauvais décorateur." Costume is too ornate, too gilded; and this is bad, for "plus les genres sont sérieux, plus il faut de sévérité dans les vêtements." In the moment of a tumultuous action, men cannot dress, says Diderot, as if it were a *jour de fête* (VII, 373-375).

The Italian actors are praised for their liberty of action; one is reminded that they pay less attention to the spectator than do the French actors. He concludes:

> On trouve, dans leur action, je ne sais quoi d'original et d'aisé, qui me plaît et qui plairait à tout le monde, sans les insipides discours et l'intrigue absurde qui le défigurent (VII, 377).

The pedantry which exists in French poetics and in their dramatic compositions will impede the progress of action or pantomime. Gesture and action should, therefore, often replace the *discours,* and there are entire scenes in which it would be more natural to move about rather than to speak (VII, 378). Diderot next takes Euripides' *Iphigenia in Tauris* and relates what he would do to enhance the movement of this tragedy: Orestes would show fear by means of his eyes and fleeting glances; his speeches would stop and then resume; there would be a certain disorder to his action; he would fall to earth, only to be raised by Pylades; the hero would remain for a moment in a state of agony and death. This action, representing a sort of pantomime, would produce great effect; even Pylades' action here would affect one much more than a *discours* (VII, 380-381). In brief, Diderot is again advocating fewer speeches and more movement, recalling to his reader

---

[12] These are the grounds on which Diderot reproaches Shakespeare: "Le défaut de Shakespeare n'est pas le plus grand dans lequel un poète puisse tomber. Il manque seulement un peu de goût." *Œuvres complètes*, VII, 374.

that the laws of picturesque composition are the same as those of pantomime (VII, 385).

Diderot's critical documents here examined were destined, of course, to promote the cause of an intermediary genre, to formulate the plan for a theater of the future, and to show later playwrights the brilliant role which they would be able to occupy in the development of dramatic art in France. So far as the moral value of the theater, scenery and costume, action, and pantomime are concerned, Diderot was transmitting essentially new ideas. [13] With each theory regarding composition, he was perhaps drawing further away from the actual creation of tragedy ressembling the genre of days past, without abandoning completely the possibility of a tragedy which somehow would acquire new forms of expression.

---

[13] Félix Gaiffe, *Le Drame en France au XVIIIe siècle* (Paris: Armand Colin, 1910), pp. 160-161.

Chapter VI

MARMONTEL

Jean-François Marmontel (1723-1799) began his education under the Jesuits and at one time even decided to enter the order of his preceptors;[1] but, sidetracked probably by his mother, who saw in him her only means of support, he went to Toulouse to continue his studies and to find employment.[2] From there, with the encouragement of Voltaire, who had received and read some of his verse, Marmontel left for Paris in 1745.[3] He was advised by the former to try a career in the theater, and the next few years were to be spent studying dramatic theory — for the most part Aristotle and Corneille — and frequenting the Théâtre-Français.[4] By 1746 Marmontel had sold a translation of Pope's *Rape of the Lock* and had won a poetry prize designated as a "prix d'Académie."[5] His first tragedy, *Denys*, was presented in February of 1748 with heartwarming acclaim, but his next three plays were to be only partially successful.[6] Marmontel quickly established himself, however, as an *homme du monde*, frequenting the home of Madame de Tencin, where he met such men as Montesquieu, Marivaux, Helvétius, and attending the gatherings held by D'Holbach, which brought him into contact with Diderot, Grimm, and

---

[1] S. Lenel, *Un Homme de lettres au XVIIIᵉ siècle. Marmontel.* (Paris: Hachette, 1902), pp. 25-26; 34.
[2] *Ibid.*, pp. 41-42.
[3] *Ibid.*, p. 48.
[4] *Ibid.*, pp. 54-55.
[5] *Ibid.*, p. 57.
[6] *Ibid.*, pp. 74-75.

other *encyclopédistes*.⁷ In November of 1763, Marmontel was elected to the Académie Française and twenty years later became its *secrétaire perpétuel*.⁸

The articles which created Marmontel's reputation as a critic appeared in the *Encyclopédie* from 1753 to 1756. From these he drew the material for a *Poétique française* (1763)⁹ and later combined all this criticism, presenting it as a body of material which he published in his *Oeuvres complètes* under the title *Eléments de littérature* (1787).¹⁰ These articles and essays, filling some four volumes, are therefore the result of thirty years of almost continuous work.¹¹ It is this criticism which we shall use for an examination of his theories and attitudes with regard to tragedy, a genre that definitely dominated his thoughts.

Marmontel explains tragic pleasure in terms of its being a true pleasure of the soul in its emotions. This pleasure stems from the natural attraction which induces us to exercise our physical and mental faculties, that is, to experience the fact that we are sensitive, intelligent, active, and alert beings. It is this same exercise of *sensibilité* which causes children to love the marvellous, even though they may be frightened by it; it is the same process which caused certain peoples of the past to attend gladiatorial combats; and it is the factor which draws more sensitive and gentle nations to the theater, where passions are portrayed. Here it is that the "grand pathétique," as Marmontel calls it, becomes terror and pity — the soul of tragedy. Tragedy is a genre which must present our fellow beings in peril and misfortune; it must be a calamity or a misfortune which touches us. It must, at the same time, give us the appearance of truth.¹²

A definite moral and didactic purpose is ascribed to tragedy by Marmontel. In his article, "Tragédie," he states that the aim of

---

⁷ S. Lenel, *op. cit.*, p. 112-113.
⁸ *Ibid.*, p. 198.
⁹ *Ibid.*, p. 364.
¹⁰ *Ibid*, p. 501.
¹¹ *Ibid.*, p. 364.
¹² Jean-François Marmontel, *Œuvres complètes* (18 vols.; Paris: Verdière, 1818-1819), XV, 381-382. Subsequent citations in parentheses refer to this edition.

this genre is the correction of mores through an imitation of them in an action which serves as an example. Without this purpose, the pleasure one gains would be only "puérile et momentané" (XII, 143; XV, 416). In another article, "Bonté," he states that the good quality of a tragedy consists of intimidating the passions, of restraining them through the use of frightening examples (XII, 362). On still another occasion, while discussing comedy, Marmontel inserts the following idea:

> La sensibilité humaine est le principe d'où part la tragédie; le pathétique en est le moyen; la crainte des passions funestes, l'horreur des grands crimes, et l'amour des sublimes vertus sont les fins qu'elle se propose (XII, 477).

In an article called "Moralité," he seeks to establish that the aim of poetry is pleasure. Citing immediately the Horatian concept of the *utile dulce*, Marmontel proceeds to state firmly that all serious poetry must have its object of utility, its moral aim. The truth of impression or thought which results, the salutary effect which pity, fear, admiration, scorn, hate, or love produces in the soul of man, is what he terms "moralité." He points out that sometimes this quality is presented directly, but most often it is left to be gathered in as an inference. This process of deduction consoles and actually deceives man's vanity, which otherwise might have been offended. This is in large part, he adds, the artifice of tragedy (XIV, 296-297).

When Jean-Jacques Rousseau's *Lettre à d'Alembert*, advocating the abolishment of the theater on moral grounds, appeared in 1758, Marmontel replied by drafting an essay which he entitled *Apologie du théâtre*. This document is actually an analysis of Rousseau's statements, which are quoted and then attacked. We summarize here some of the principal features of Marmontel's defense of the theater.

Answering Rousseau's charges that the theater does not have the power to change one's convictions or mores, Marmontel replies by using Racine's *Britannicus* as the basis of his rebuttal:

> S'il n'y avait à la cour que des Narcisses, Britannicus n'y serait point souffert; s'il n'y avait que des Burrhus, Britannicus y serait inutile; mais il y a des hommes vague-

ment ambitieux et irrésolus encore, ou mal affermis dans la route qu'ils doivent suivre; c'est pour ceux-là que Britannicus est une leçon, et n'est point une insulte (X, 177-178).

Marmontel does concede the fact that the theater is not a school for the republic; but it is a school for its citizens, a place where "les vices épars et les passions isolées" can be attacked, even if the fundamental mores of a political constitution cannot. Marmontel recalls that Corneille wrote for his century, consulting the taste of his century. He authorized, for example, the duel which occurs in the *Cid*, but the main question concerns the honor of Don Diègue. The Cid's act, therefore, becomes one of virtue (X, 179-180).

In other statements Marmontel indicates his conviction that the frightening examples furnished by tragedy inspire terror, pity, and fear, while such qualities as ambition and love are depicted as either odious or interesting, according to the circumstances which cause them to be virtuous or criminal. "Telle est la règle invariable de la scène tragique; et le poëte qui l'aurait violée, révolterait tous les esprits" (X, 182-183). At the end of *Cinna*, *Athalie*, and *Alzire*, for example, it is not the taste for vice which is aroused; nor is love shown to be vicious. At the conclusion of *Phèdre*, it is not the crime we detest less (as Rousseau had contended); it is the criminal character who becomes personal in our minds, and we feel compassion for her as a fellow human being; "ce retour sur nous-mêmes, qui est le principe de la pitié, est aussi celui de la crainte" (X, 189-190). Out of a hundred tragedies, there is not one, states Marmontel, which shows interest in favor of the crime (X, 194-195). Unlike Rousseau, he feels that we must know that man caught in the excess of passion is capable of everything, and thereby we can learn to detest this passion. This becomes, then, the actual aim and object of tragedy (X, 200).

In the *Eléments* an elevated, lofty idea of the theater accompanies its moral purpose. It is the tone of tragedy which is to be grand; its language is to be more sustained and noble and its pronunciation more distinguished than in everyday society, where communication is carried on at closer range. Marmontel warns, however, about "the proportions of perspective":

> ... c'est-à-dire de manière que l'expression de la voix soit réduite au degré de la nature, lorsqu'elle parvient à l'oreille des spectateurs. Voilà dans l'un et l'autre genre, la seule exagération qui soit permise: tout ce qui l'excède est vicieux (XIII, 25-26).

The principle of all the arts which attempt to imitate nature is the idea that the imitation must be "quelque chose de ressemblant et non pas de semblable." It is by virtue of this theory that tragedy is an expression in verse, employing a more elevated tone than would ever be found in nature (XV, 179-181). On another occasion, however, Marmontel suggests that the language of these characters of high rank, in order to be true, must be closer to nature than "celui du poëte inspiré par un dieu." Sophocles and Euripides recognized this factor, and Greek tragedy became less poetic, less artificial than it currently is among the French tragedians. The *pathétique* was a more dominant element in the theater of the ancients, and a naturalness of expression gave it more force. Racine did not approach this naturalness, but never did a poet make a more harmonious mixture of ordinary and poetic language (XV, 321-322).

The characteristics of ancient tragedy are further defined in Marmontel's article entitled "Tragédie." Here he elaborates on the system of modern tragedy as opposed to that of the ancients. He begins by explaining that man falls into peril and misfortune either through a cause beyond his control ("hors de lui") or through an inherent one ("en lui-même.") This "hors de lui" is of course one's destiny, the accidents of life, or the action which the gods exercise over man. The "en lui-même" would then refer to his own weakness, his imprudence, his passions or vices, and even sometimes his virtues. For Marmontel, the distinction between these two conditions accounts for the two systems of tragedy, the ancient and the modern. We, the moderns, continues Marmontel, have taken the ancients' subjects which present a main character whose misfortune is caused by "une cause étrangère," and have added "une plénitude et une continuité d'action, une gradation d'intérêt, un enchaînement de situations, un développement de moeurs, de sentiments, de caractères, un art et des ressorts inconnus aux anciens" (XV, 384). The moderns have made tragedy, moreover, not a view of man as a slave of destiny, but a picture of him as a slave of his passions. Thus the mainspring of modern tragic action, since the time of Corneille, its creator, has been in the heart of man (XV, 383-386).

Continuing his development of this particular theory, Marmontel divides Greek tragedy into categories: *pathétique, morale, simple,* and *implexe.* Modern tragedy, which employs a system of passions either portrayed simply or combined with the workings of destiny, has three divisions: a type in which the main character is responsible for his own misfortune, as is Roxane; a type depicting the main character in conflict with evil beings, as we see Britannicus; a kind which presents an unfortunate being, who must choose between duty and desire, or at least between contrary interests. Rodrigue, Zaïre, and Inès de Castro are examples of the latter. As mentioned above, Marmontel finds that the ancient system of tragedy was more *pathétique,* since man was a slave of a will not his own; he was the plaything of an unjust power. The ancient system was, therefore, easier to manipulate than is the modern; for among the Greeks, for example, there had to be no accounting for the decrees of destiny (XV, 387-390). This idea of fatality better suited the spaciousness of their theaters; and like a picture intended to be seen from a distance, the tragic events springing from external sources simplified everything (XV, 393).

Nuance, however, and not simplification was needed for the depiction of the passions; the delicate touches of modern tragedy would be lost in the wide scope of the Greek theater (XV, 394). All these workings of the human heart lead Marmontel to conclude that the modern system is richer and more fruitful. It is the contrast of passions in the modern tragic theater which furnishes a variety of situations and a great number of "mouvements" unknown to the ancients. It is this contrast, also this flux and reflux of the passions which have complicated the problem to be solved in French tragedy (XIII, 370; XIV, 160). In the final analysis, however, the new system is more universal; for the system of the passions, as Marmontel refers to it, belongs to all countries and to all centuries. The French theater has become, in effect, "le tableau du monde" (XV, 399-401).

The passions, having become almost the cornerstone of Marmontel's system of modern tragedy, are now directly related to his discussion of tragic character. The essential qualities of the "caractère intéressant" are listed as candor, nobleness, greatness of soul, rectitude, and *sensibilité*. If a passion has made him unjust, he must recognize this fact. Weakness may be exhibited as part of his character, but never falseness or ambition; never envy, violence, nor cruelty. He is, nevertheless, a mixture of good and evil, according to Aristotelian requirement; and all his passions mus carry with them "une sorte d'excuse et d'apologie, qui le fasse plaindre d'en être le victime, et qui empêche de le haïr" (XV, 410-411). Thus it is not a question of making the passions hated, but rather of causing them to be feared. They are to be shown as a mixture of good and evil, just as they are seen in nature. The goodness and virtue of the main character will only cause one to feel more strongly the danger of the passion which has brought about the hero's downfall. At this point, Marmontel reiterates the idea that the language of the passions would be lost under the mask of the Greek actor and in the immensity of his theater (XV, 412; XIII, 393).

Of all the active passions, Marmontel holds that love is the most theatrical, the most interesting, "la plus féconde en tableaux pathétiques, la plus utile à voir dans ses redoutables excès" (XV, 413). Paternal and maternal love, treasures of the ancient theater, were neglected by the modern playwright until the advent of Voltaire, who first inserted this "tendresse du sang" into modern subjects. Perhaps it is he who deserves to be placed above Corneille and Racine as having best known the workings of the human heart (XV, 414-415). Rather than reproach French dramatic poets for their use of love in tragedy, Marmontel finds that they have discovered in its various movements an inexhaustible source of the finest poetry (XIII, 277). The simple malady of love, however, is not tragic. It is a passion which must be complicated, and this is why Marmontel pronounces *Bérénice* a weaker tragedy than *Inès de Castro* (XV, 425). Love can also be rendered eloquent, as can all the other passions, by an element which he calls *douleur*. This passion (and he refers to it as such) is capable of converting every type of character into a pathetic being (XIII, 280).

According to Marmontel, theatrical illusion "consiste à faire oublier ce qu'on sait, pour ne penser qu'à ce qu'on voit" (XII, 125). In tragedy, where truth counts for nothing, and *vraisemblance* is all-important, illusion is never complete, nor should it be. We never forget the actor, and forever aware that what he is doing is a "jeu," we exclaim, says Marmontel, in the midst of a very moving scene, about the merits of his acting. We are therefore not applauding Augustus, but instead we are paying homage to the actor performing the role. There are times when such a thing as full or complete illusion would be revolting or painful; furthermore, if the illusion were complete, the admiration we feel for the superiority of the painting to the model would be lost (XIV, 92). Marmontel believes that when one attends a play, two thoughts are present. One of these is the actual truth which is perceived: you have come to see a performance, the action in reality is taking place in a theater, the people surrounding you have come for the same purpose as you, and the scenery which you are looking at is painted and fully imaginary. The other thought present is the idea of actual illusion. Thus the task of the dramatic poet, the actor, and the set designer is that of strengthening the impression of *vraisemblance* and weakening the idea of reality. Nature, Marmontel points out, has a thousand details that would be true, but they lack interest, *agrément*, or *décence*. The element sought after in the theater is "une nature exquise, curieuse, et intéressante." The illusion must, therefore, be lively and strong. In this way, the spectator is not so free to think; for once thought and reflexion take over, illusion is destroyed. The powerful illusion, the forceful imitation might be too horribly true (XIV, 95-98), and this is where the question of *bienséance* must be considered.

Marmontel finds that *bienséance* is related to the spectator, while *convenance* has connection with the character. When the dramatist has his creation act the way he would have acted and spoken in his particular period of history, *convenance* has been observed. If, however, the mores of that era are shocking for the present age, then *bienséance* will be violated, unless certain soft touches are added to their depiction. If an imitation which is too faithful offends our modesty or refinement, *décence* has been rejected. Thus, says Marmontel, to observe more closely these two principles, *bienséance* and *décence,* one is often obliged to leave behind *convenance* by altering the truth of his drama. *Bienséance,* therefore, varies according to time and place; and this is easily understandable when one consults the history of the theater. In Corneille's *Clitandre,* as Marmontel points out, Caliste actually appears in the bedroom of her *amant* when she wishes to see him. It is the progress of taste, the culture of the mind, the ideas on *politesse* of the particular society which determine and decide what constitutes *bienséance* (XII, 350-352). Certain vices are not to be exposed on the stage; but Marmontel believes that by veiling certain of these, it would be possible to employ in a useful way examples of misfortune and mistake caused by these vicious elements (XII, 364). This does not mean that blood must flow or that drunkenness be displayed on the stage, for the poetic imitation must please not only the multitude, but also the most cultivated of minds. The imitation should remain "décente, ingénieuse, exquise, digne en un mot, qu'une raison perfectionnée et un sentiment délicat en chérissent l'illusion" (XIV, 98).

Throughout the *Eléments,* Marmontel evidences an interest in the epic, relating it many times to tragedy. He finds that the former genre has the advantage of not being limited; whereas in tragedy, the poet is faced with physical and temporal restrictions. The movement of tragedy is an accelerated one, as it moves from act to act, and there is a certain anxiety and uneasiness which is fomented, a pity and fear so pressing that episodes are greatly reduced. Tragedy, like a torrent, must either break or clear the obstacles which stand in its way; while the epic, "un fleuve majestueux qui suit sa pente," is prolonged by a thousand detours. Tragedy, therefore, shows its advantage over the epic in the matter of rapidity, vehemence, and pathos of action, although the epic must be considered superior in so far as grandeur and majesty are concerned. Marmontel recalls Aristotle's statement with regard to the scope and verse form, which the author of the *Poetics* considers the epic's distinguishing features. Marmontel also notes that Tasso felt that the marvellous was the epic's only source of pathos, while tragedy employs terror and pity to achieve a creation which elicits something other than cold admiration (XII, 130-136). Later Marmontel asserts, contrary to Tasso, that the *pathétique* is the soul of tragedy, the same as it is for the epic

(XIII, 359). The dramatic poem in general requires that its author have more circumspection and discretion, since the only *bienséances* to be observed in the epic are those of language (XII, 532).

A substantial section of the *Eléments* is devoted to a discussion of the unities. Marmontel first separates unity of action from simplicity of action and proceeds to show what constitutes duplicity of action:

> Si l'épisode est absolument inutile au nœud ou au dénouement de l'action, comme l'amour de Thésée et celui de Philoctete dans nos deux *Œdipes,* et comme l'amour d'Antiochus dans la *Bérénice* de Racine, il fait duplicité d'action... (XV, 448)

Marmontel also establishes that it is not necessary that the element of desire, of fear, or hope in a tragedy be focused on a single person, but rather on one point. Thus the event, which is either feared or sought after, can concern a family or perhaps an entire nation (XV, 449). He suggests with regard to the unity of time, that it would be more desirable for the action (Marmontel calls it "la durée fictive de l'action") to limit itself to the time required for the presentation. He decides, however, that one becomes an enemy of the arts and of the pleasure which they grant when laws depriving them of their rich, inventive quality are imposed. Marmontel then speaks of the tacit agreement the public maintains with the poet, who may use these freedoms so long as they please and touch the spectator. So it is that the *entr'acte* may be used to extend the time to twenty-four hours, which then becomes "le temps fictif de l'action." Our critic does not recommend, however, that this liberty be carried to excess, as illustrated by the practice of the English and the Spanish. If a fines subject requires it, the dramatist can assume that more than one day has passed. Marmontel notes that the Greeks sometimes violated the unity of place, as seen, for example, in the *Eumenides*. As for the French, he does not regard the changing of place as a licence or an abuse. The *entr'acte* means that there is an absence of actors and spectators, and thus the characters in the play are able to have moved their location in the process of going from one act to the other. The spectators, Marmontel declares, have no fixed spot, and if the action changes, they change with it.

To fall within the laws of *vraisemblance*, however, the action must be moved during the interval separating the acts, and not between scenes. As stated above, the longest duration that can be given the *entr'acte* is one day or one night; this determines, therefore, the distance to which the scene of the action can be carried (XV, 452-455).

Considering the *récit* under the heading of narration, Marmontel determines that the character who delivers it must, first of all, instruct and persuade. Thus its primary characteristics are those of clarity and *vraisemblance*. If there is obscurity in the recital of facts, this must be so only for the characters on the stage (XIV, 326-327). The recit must also be *à propos*. The account of Hippolyte's death in the *récit de Théramène* is given, for example, at the wrong moment. Thésée, "dans le premier accès de sa douleur," is not ready to receive the description. As a test of the *récit's* opportuneness, the writer must therefore put himself in the place of the one receiving the facts to determine if he would be attentive at the chosen moment (XIV, 332-333). The *récit*, moreover, cannot neglect certain details; but there are descriptions and fine lines of poetry, as seen in Théramène's *récit*, which are out of place. It is of little concern to Thésée that the sea monster has horns or that his body is covered with scales. The intention of the one who narrates or recounts is to be one of instruction, with also the purpose of perhaps moving the auditor. In addition, the dramatic poet should remember that the *récit* pronounced by the actor who is calm needs more ornamentation than the one which is to compose an impassioned speech (XIV, 341-344).

Marmontel, like Voltaire and Diderot, is cognizant of the fact that the resources of his era open to the dramatist, so far as *décor* and costume are concerned, are very slight. He also recognizes this scarcity as the attributing factor in the lack of action in French tragedy and the abundance of *discours*. The spoken word, Marmontel admits, is often a weak and slow expression, but one must at least offer to the ears that which cannot be given to the eyes. The lack of decoration in the tragic theater carries with it, he decides, the impossibility of change and thereby limits the dramatic author to the unity of place in its strictest sense. This can be viewed, of course, as something of a contradiction of his above statement concerning this unity, or as a realization of the difficulty inherent in conciliating theory and practice. Marmontel also attacks the poor costuming of the actors, speaking of it in terms of "indécence". Here it is a question of opposing established usage and exposing one's self to the danger of innovation. In this respect, he praises Mademoiselle Clairon [13] for being the first to wear a costume "du pays et du temps" (XIII, 49-53).

In speaking of denouement, Marmontel refers his reader to a perfect example, which is found in *Rodogune;* for here the action "longtemps balancé dans cette alternative, tient l'âme des spectateurs incertaine et flottante jusqu'à son achèvement" (XIII, 102). The art of the denouement consists in preparing it without actually announcing it. To prepare it means that the action has been arranged so that what precedes it, produces it. Marmontel is obviously drawing from Aristotle on this point, and he does not hide the fact. Interest in the denouement is maintained only through uncertainty; through this quality the soul is suspended between fear and hope, and from the mixture of the two, interest is fostered. Marmontel finds that the choice between the probable and the necessary, which Aristotle seems to leave to the discretion of the poet so far as bringing about the change of fortune, is not to be taken as a steadfast rule. He explains:

> Un dénouement qui n'est que vraisemblable n'en exclut aucun de possible, et entretient l'incertitude en les laissant tous imaginer. Un dénouement nécessaire ne peut laisser prévoir que lui; et l'on ne doit pas espérer qu'un succès infaillible, ou qu'un revers inévitable échappe aux yeux des spectateurs (XIII, 102-103).

The more the spectators give themselves over to the action, the more their attention is directed toward its conclusion; and once the end is foreseen, the action is ended.

Marmontel continues his discussion of denouement by listing what he considers its four types. There is the *pathétique*, in which the good succumb to the purposes of the wicked, but which leaves

---

[13] The reference to Mademoiselle Clairon concerns her appearance in Voltaire's *L'Orphelin de la Chine.*

us with a grief we do not care to feel; another type, which depicts good fortune for the crime, but not necessarily bad result for the innocent party; a third type, which employs the idea of fatality and which shows no "moralité"; a fourth kind, which shows innocence menaced and persecuted, but which presents it issuing forth triumphant, either through the idea of fatality or the action of men. Each of these types is lacking the idea of the *pathétique* or the conception of *moralité;* and to be perfect, Marmontel suggests that a tragedy be *morale* and *pathétique* (XIII, 106-107). Thus he suggests a *dénouement heureux*,[14] although he would have us believe that Aristotle seemed to forbid such a thing. Here the hero leaves the abyss into which his passion has led him, and the spectator senses relief when he sees his deliverance; he feels the moral purpose of the drama, because the passion, which is the cause of the danger, has had time to create its impression of fear (XIII, 108).

Marmontel regards pantomime as a natural effect of dramatic action, but he quickly concludes that it does not constitute action. He finds that these movements, these *tableaux,* this "jeu de théâtre" are independent of real dramatic action, a type of beauty which finds its seat in the soul of the actors (XII, 139). The impressions made by means of the ear may be slower, he says, but they are possibly deeper and more lasting. The eyes introduce only sensations while the ears transmit thought. Therefore this element called "l'action pantomime" speaks only to the eyes, and a role like that of Phèdre is not made for the eyes. It serves, however, as an example of "le sublime et le propre de l'action"; once this sort of role is reduced to pantomime, the only result achieved is one which touches on the ordinary or the commonplace (XII,

---

[14] While stating that Aristotle required the *dénouement funeste*, Marmontel presents an interpretation of catharsis: "Son object moral [Aristote's] n'était pas de modérer en nous les passions actives, mais d'habituer l'âme aux impressions de la terreur et de la pitié, de l'en charger comme d'un poids qui exerçât ses forces, et lui fît paraître plus léger le poids de ses propres malheurs ... Sans donc s'occuper de l'émotion que nous cause le progrès des événements, Aristote s'attache à celle que le spectacle laisse dans nos âmes; c'est par là, dit-il, que la tragédie purge la crainte, la pitié, et toutes les passions semblables, c'est-à-dire toutes les affections douloureuses qui nous viennent du dehors." *Œuvres complètes,* XII, 391-392.

141-142). Gesture does not express a chain of circumstances or events which evidence either the danger of our passions or the ridicule of our weaknesses. Marmontel further reinforces the moral aim of the theater with the following statement:

> Le spectacle n'est qu'un moyen de l'éloquence poétique; et quoique son objet immédiat soit d'amuser, de plaire, d'émouvoir, ce n'est point encore là sa fin ultérieure; cette fin est de renvoyer le spectateur plus éclairé, plus sage, meilleur, s'il est possible, au moins plus riche de pensées et de sentiments vertueux (XII, 144-145).

There is in the *Eléments* an excellent defense of verse as a means of theatrical expression. Marmontel indicates, first of all, that there is an advantage to be found in the cadence of poetry, and an advantage in so far as memorization for the actor is concerned. The actor is aided in recalling his lines, as one *hémistiche* leads to another. In tragedy, especially,

> tout n'est pas également passionné: il y a des éclaircissements, des développements, des passages inévitables d'une situation à l'autre; il y a des délibérations tranquilles, en un mot, des moments de calme, où, n'étant pas assez émue par l'intérêt de la chose, l'âme demande à être occupée du charme de l'expression, pour ne pas cesser de jouir. C'est alors que le coloris de la poésie doit enchanter l'imagination, que l'harmonie du vers doit enchanter l'oreille... (XV, 433)

Prose has the charm of naturalness and *vérité,* but one does not search for "la vérité toute nue" in the theater. One seeks a truth which is embellished. The dramatic illusion is never complete, for we know that we are to be deceived, and we are prepared for such, "pourvu que ce soit avec agrément, et le plus d'agrément possible." The artifice of the language, therefore, is one of the accessories which tempers the illusion, which does not, however, alter the naturalness of thought and feeling (XV, 431-435).

Despite his defense of poetry, Marmontel does recognize that the alexandrine is monotonous. He attributes this to two factors: dramatic authors have not worked hard enough with the possibility of varying the caesura;[15] the rhymes fall two by two, and with the periodic return of these two final sounds repeated a thousand times, the ear becomes tired. As a matter of reform, Marmontel advocates a *rime croisée*, with a variation in rhythm, using an alternating eight and twelve-syllable line. The secret of varying the harmony and movement of the alexandrine will be found "dans la coupe des phrases et dans l'heureux mélange des incises et des périodes." This is a secret to be learned by reading good poets such as Racine and Voltaire (XII, 172-174). In a later article Marmontel praises these two dramatists and includes Corneille in his statement:

> En général, la grande manière de versifier c'est de penser en masse, et de remplir chaque vers d'une portion de la pensée, à peu près comme un sculpteur prend ses dimensions... C'est la manière de Corneille, de Racine, de Voltaire, et de tous ceux dont les idées ont coulé à pleine source. Les autres ont produit les leurs, pour ainsi dire goutte à goutte... (XIII, 166)

Marmontel, the critic, is truly a representative of what Saintsbury call the "middle state."[16] He represents, that is, "an eclectic, loosely articulated view of literature, in which many current motifs of literary theory are juxtaposed: rationalism, neo-classicism, the new historical sense, the cult for taste and genius."[17] Marmontel draws heavily on such celebrated theorists as Aristotle, Horace, Vida, Scaliger, and Boileau;[18] but then on frequent occasions, he veers from this path to present new directions in dramatic theory. Although he does not dismiss the idea of verse in the tragic theater, his attitudes towards the alexandrine reflect his innovational leanings. Unattracted by pantomime and action in tableau form, he is, however, infected by the idea of the *pathétique* and the *morale*,[19] which so greatly captivated France in the

---

[15] Marmontel quotes a line from *Phèdre* to give an example of variation: "Voilà mon cœur. C'est là que ta main doit frapper." *Ibid.*, XII, 173.

[16] George E. B. Saintsbury, *A History of Criticism and Literary Taste in Europe* (3 vols.; New York: Dodd Mead and Co., 1902), II, 525.

[17] René Wellek, *A History of Modern Criticism: 1750-1950* (4 vols.; New Haven: Yale University Press, 1955), I, 66.

[18] Saintsbury, II, 526.

[19] *Ibid.*, p. 526.

last half of the eighteenth century. Recognizing the need for improvements in *décor* and costume, he remains, at the same time, a critic who comprehends the evocative, more permanent resources of the spoken word. Marmontel's taste, at least in practice, is Voltaire's;[20] as such, he remains historically interesting and at many times exceedingly stimulating.

---

[20] Wellek, I, 65.

CHAPTER VII

LOUIS-SÉBASTIEN MERCIER

Louis-Sébastien Mercier (1740-1814), a Parisian by birth,[1] demonstrated an almost precocious interest in the theater and in the other literary expressions of his age. Frequenter of the Café Procope, acquaintance of Crébillon père and the Abbé Prévost, he launched his literary career in 1760 with the publication of some *héroïdes,* a poetic genre very much in vogue at the time. Destiny, at least for the moment, was to make a teacher of him; and in 1763, Mercier left for Bordeaux to accept a position at the Collège de la Madeleine, where, in spite of everything, he did not abandon his aspirations for fame in the literary world. Mercier's first critical work, *Le Bonheur des gens de lettres,* appeared this same year, exhibiting the young man's literary orthodoxy, which allowed him, as he said, "de pleurer avec Racine et de rire avec Molière."[2] The reading of the *Nouvelle Héloïse* and the study of English literature opened to him, however, new influences. Rousseau became Mercier's master and Shakespeare a respected artist. In 1765, he resigned his duties at the *collège* to devote himself entirely to literature.[3]

Besides the poetry mentioned above, Mercier's scope of literary creation includes the composition of academic discourses (*éloges*);[4] *drames* and critical prefaces; social, political, philosoph-

---

[1] Léon Béclard, *Sébastien Mercier* (Paris: Champion, 1903), p. 2.
[2] *Ibid.,* pp. 10-18.
[3] *Ibid.,* pp. 23-26.
[4] *Ibid.,* pp. 40-41.

ical and critical works. To the decade of the seventies belong his novel, *l'An 2440* (1770), and his most important item of dramatic criticism, the *Du théâtre, ou Nouvel essai sur l'art dramatique* (1773). This latter work was followed five years later by a reiterative document, the *Nouvel examen de la tragédie française*. Other critical attitudes pertinent to drama are to be found in *Mon bonnet de nuit* (1784) and in the twelve-volume *Tableau de Paris* (1781-88).[5]

Mercier's reaction to French tragedy is a vehement one, quickly asserting itself as iconoclastic, and redoubling at most every instant, with attack upon attack. He finds that the French theater in general, "gothiquement conçu dans un siècle à demi barbare, enfant du hasard et rejetton [sic] parasite,"[6] has conserved the imprint of its ludicrous origin. Almost like a graft taken from another land, it has been transplanted by rude and unskilled hands. He speaks of the servile imitators — "défricheurs," as he dubs them — who knew neither the mores of the ancients, nor the usages of the moderns. They did not know what to borrow from the ancients, and they had no conception of what to add to their sources (p. viii). Such men as Jodelle, Garnier, Hardy, and Rotrou, in reviving ancient subjects, disfigured the Greek background. Those who followed these writers left behind what Mercier recognizes as the same dialogue, the same procedure, the same denouements; the dramatic authors were guilty at the same time of creating more words and *discours* than action.[7] In short, the tragedian has remained a *copiste*, composing in his library and not "dans le livre ouvert du monde" (p. ix).

---

[5] W. W. Pusey, *Louis-Sébastien Mercier in Germany* (New York: Columbia University Press, 1939), pp. 6-18.

[6] Louis-Sébastien Mercier, *Du théâtre ou Nouvel essai sur l'art dramatique* (Amsterdam: E. Van Harrevelt, 1773), p. vii. Citations in parentheses refer to this edition.

[7] In *Mon bonnet de nuit* (4 vols.; Neuchâtel: De l'Imprimerie de la Société Typographique, 1784), III, 239-240, Mercier again accuses French dramatists of "l'esprit servile," of their ridiculous adherence to childish and absurd rules; in the *Tableau de Paris* (12 vols.; Amsterdam, 1782-1788), IV, 69, he assumes the same tone, accusing the French theater of uniformity, of "la ressemblance de ces plans étroits," of its "caractères répétés." The *Nouvel examen de la tragédie française* (Yverdun, 1778), p. 100, censures French tragedy for its uniformity of peripeteia, for conformity in language, and for its excessive number of tirades. This last reference is cited by Béclard, p. 179.

The foundation of the French theater is, therefore, vicious and ridiculous, and the superb French tragedy one speaks of is nothing more than "un fantôme revêtu de pourpre et d'or, mais qui n'a aucune réalité" (p. ix). Invention becomes Mercier's cry, as he calls for the forsaking of models which, heretofore, have been the basis of imitation. The rules, the poetics have ruined the most inventive minds. Dramatic authors have not traveled their way alone; instead, they have used a map, and, thereby, have seen things in exactly the same way as their predecessors (pp. xii-xiii).

What Mercier finds pernicious in French tragedy is soon defined:

> ... c'est cette grandeur imaginaire qu'on a soin de rehausser encore, c'est cette existence surnaturelle qu'on enfle, en passant même les bornes qu'elle s'est données; ce sont ces vers orgueilleux qui déifiant les rois, insultent à la misère de la multitude; ce sont ces crimes qui n'ont pas même été commis et que l'on invente à loisir pour flétrir mon imagination et me faire détester la condition humaine (pp. 36-37).

He also lambastes poor costuming [8] in the theater, and then turns to speak against Corneille's "intrigues amoureuses," which disfigure his finest plays. Racine employed all his art to turn his heroes into Frenchmen; Mercier finds that this latter playwright is characterized by monotony, since almost all his characters have the same physiognomy (pp. 42-43).

According to Mercier, French tragedy is founded, almost always, not on history, but on some obscure historical point. It takes only a line of history to suffice, and, moreover, "un songe, une reconnaissance, un billet, un soulèvement, un coup de théâtre, ont bâti grand nombre de pièces" (pp. 45-46). Only a philosopher should study history, for the ambitious man consults it to seek justification for his injustices, while the tyrant simply becomes more wicked by examining it. History in French tragedy has been denaturated, and "il n'y a point eu de gouvernement sur

---

[8] Cf. Mercier, *Tableau de Paris*, III, 15-16.

la terre, auquel on puisse assigner rigoureusement la plus exacte de nos tragédies" (p. 48).

An advocate of the *drame*, Mercier, as one might suspect, is critically retreating from the idea of the genre which we accept as tragedy. On one occasion in particular, his comments seem pertinent to our study. He sees that the sharp distinction between tragedy and comedy

> ... a sûrement été très funeste à l'art. Le poète, qui a fait une tragédie, s'est cru dans l'obligation d'être toujours tendu, sérieux, imposant; il a dédaigné ces détails qui pouvaient être nobles, quoique communs, ces grâces simples, ce naturel qui vivifie un ouvrage et lui donne les couleurs vraies (p. 95).

The idea that tragedy should make one cry has brought to the stage unforeseen, unexpected deaths. Rhetorically, Mercier asks if the French, left only with the tragedies of Corneille and Racine, would know the mores, the character, the genius of their nation and century; the details of their "vie privée." Would one know what virtues were the most esteemed? Would one discover the *tableau* of actual mores? (p. 103).

As for the rules which govern the dramatist, Mercier accepts the following as the most difficult and the most important: "Gardez-vous d'offrir une action qui ne soit pas vraisemblable" (p. 144). The unity of time,[9] as a rule, is flexible, and the dramatist is certainly allowed to exceed thirty hours if necessary. The unity of place is the least respectable of all, but he asserts that the unity of interest (so much in the minds of the critic and the playwright since the advent of La Motte) is due reverence. Adherence to this precept will assure the dramatic poet of attention from the spectator; it is a rule which will permit no distraction, but which will serve to connect the author and his work directly to the unity of action. It is to be accepted, therefore, as the only essential unity (pp. 145-147).

---

[9] It has been noted, says Mercier, that "nos vingt-quatre heures n'avaient servi qu'à accumuler grossièrement les invraisemblances les plus ineptes et les plus bizarres." *Ibid.*, IV, 170.

Mercier speaks of another rule which he terms ridiculous. This is the one which calls for a play, especially a tragedy, to be composed of five acts. Our critic refers to Aristotle, stating that the Greek theorist did not invent this law, and that, moreover, in the works of Sophocles and Euripides, we do not see these forced interruptions. "Intermèdes," as Mercier calls the divisions within the play, should be placed "selon l'étendue de l'action et d'après le besoin." He finally lays the responsibility for the five-act rule at the feet of Horace, who remains, in his eyes, its authority. Mercier would prefer, however, to follow the example of Sophocles and Euripides; for Horace, like Boileau, never knew how to draw up the plan for a scene (pp. 252-253).

Corneille's adherence to the rules is explained. The author of *Horace* lived in an age when one loved "les difficultés vaincues," in an epoch when the French nation imprisoned its mind within the limits of a sonnet or a *rondeau*. Corneille, we are reminded, was very superstitious with regard to the established rules; he was a timid legislator, a dramatist who "a mal vu l'art dans lequel il a excellé." No matter how great Corneille may have been, concludes Mercier, "il fut esclave des idées dominantes" (p. 255).

Unfriendly and diffident so far as the rules are concerned, Mercier also displays a hostile attitude towards verse and rhyme. He decides that the alexandrine is "lourd, pesant," that it produces an eternal monotony. French poetry in general does not have the grace, the ease, the free and moving proudness of ancient poetry. Prose, because of its flexibility, simplicity, and attractiveness will make more of an impression in the field of the drama; and besides, it is generally read more and is capable of the nobility and vehemence found in the finest verse (pp. 296-297).

With regard to the subject of rhyme, Mercier is even more rabid. The dramatic author, he feels, should seek precise and rigorous expression rather than rhyme. He says that all poets consider rhyme as an integral part of poetry, while in reality, rhyme has become poetry's ridicule and scourge. Rhyme is guilty of other crimes:

> Cette rime tyranique, cette ritournelle de consonnances, ce tintement puéril font perdre à la langue sa netteté, sa précision, sa flexibilité même. Cette coupe gênante étrangle les pensées, et par là le style devient uniforme

et hâché. La prose la plus commune a un caractère plus libre, et plaît davantage à tout homme sensé.[10]

Mercier further describes rhyme as "ce joug barbare," a fetter which the English and Italians have cast aside. Now is the time for French poets to free themselves from this unbearable monotony. Thought, continues Mercier, is sacrificed to rhyme; he judges that rhyme often renders Corneille diffuse and unintelligible, and causes Racine to be hidden constantly behind his characters; even in the tumult of unbridled passion produced in the works of this latter poet, Mercier hears "sa flûte douce qui cadence des périodes arrondies."[11] The poet is never lost from view. Rhyme is also considered to be something of a paradox, for it is a conventional beauty which destroys beauties otherwise "plus vives, plus précieuses, et plus naturelles." Rhyme is, therefore, a false ornament, one suitable for the *chanson* and the *vaudeville*.[12]

Into his attack on French tragedy and its more significant traditions and principles, Mercier incorporates a sweeping, derisive statement concerning poetics and theory. He believes Aristotle, Horace, Vida, and Boileau to be useless; that is, in relation to the theater. He states that Aristotle's *Poetics* has come down to us "tronquée et imparfaite," that it does not add any new ideas to those already evidenced by the work of Sophocles and Euripides; in fact, the unity of action had been put into practice before Aristotle prescribed it. Mercier recalls that Aristotle excludes from the theater the character who is completely virtuous, and he is precisely the one who should be exhibited on the stage. Mercier also credits Aristotle with the idea that a famous person becomes the basis of an interesting action, and then proceeds to label this a foolish concept (pp. 265-266).

Mercier admits, like Voltaire, that he does not understand Aristotelian catharsis. He deems it necessary to cure only vicious passions, and this can be done only through the fortifying powers of pity and compassion, and through the perfection of a moral sense which warns us about the noble and just elements present,

---

[10] Mercier, VIII, *op. cit.*, pp. 287-288.
[11] *Ibid.*, p. 290.
[12] *Ibid.*, pp. 290-292.

and which causes tears to flow on behalf of the misfortune. He concludes with this statement:

> C'est en développant ce que nous avons de meilleur en notre être, que le théâtre, par ses peintures vives et variées, nous offre tous les trésors de la morale, et nous enrichit de toutes les sensations exquises que produit la pitié (p. 269).

Although Mercier rejects in a rather general fashion the orthodoxy of Aristotle, he does find that they both agree that beauty consists of order and movement; that a dramatic personage should approach the general character of man (p. 268).

Mercier next attacks Horace's *Ars Poetica,* a work which he considers inferior to the *Poetics* of Aristotle. For Mercier, Horace's ideas reflect the monstrous character of the Roman theater, and his theory is typified by bad taste. Mercier is convinced, for example, that Horace should have decreed the abolishment of the chorus, an element in tragedy which our critic refers to as "invraisemblable." Mercier refuses to accept, moreover, the idea that art is as necessary as genius for the composition of poetry. Homer, Sophocles, and Euripides, we are again told, did not need a poetics to form their artistry; instead they simply served as a model for the rules (pp. 271-274).

Boileau is commended for his explanation of *bon sens* and for the composition of some excellent lines found in the *Art poétique.* Mercier says his views are just, but narrow, and that his theory stands as "un écho servile d'Horace." Boileau is further criticized for his cold manner and for a general character or temperament which alienates him from the language of the passions. He would not have understood *Zaïre,* continues Mercier, and he would surely have condemned *Rhadamiste.* To complete his *esquisse* of the theorists, Mercier exhorts the reader — especially the young — to read Diderot and Marmontel, two critics preferable to all others (pp. 276-281).

From his characterization of the theater of ancient Greece, and from his view of English drama, we find more material to affirm Mercier's attitude of scorn and his general tone of reform. The Greeks, he remarks, presented recent events on their stage; and there was naturalness in their theater, more than is found in modern drama. In using from the Greeks their dreams, their oaths, their oracles, and their fatalism as devices and elements, the French, at the same time, have omitted the finest characteristics (pp. 19-20). They have corrupted these ancient subjects by including the modern traditions and principles (p. 22). Mercier speaks of the English theater in terms of eloquence, vehemence, frankness, and its unusual interest. He also discovers the following:

> C'est chez elle [the English stage] que l'on rencontre cette vérité naïve qui produit une ressemblance parfaite: c'est le trait du cœur humain arraché sans art et sans effort, et mis au jour sans étude et sans choix (p. 207).

The English often forget *décence,* but they compensate for this fault by their ability to depict powerful scenes, and their capacity to reflect a certain boldness and vigor.

Mercier's special attraction to Shakespeare [13] is evidenced by several statements in his criticism. He groups the English playwright with Aeschylus and then suggests that if genius, as proud and independent as they, had founded the French theater, then narrow limits would have been forgotten and a wide circumference traced (p. 256). Referring to *Julius Caesar,* Mercier finds that the battle scene of Act V is almost impossible to execute; but when a man of genius has composed his work "d'après les grands tableaux que le sujet ordonne," it is not his fault if the technical resources of the theater cannot respond to the author's magnificent plan. At least Shakespeare's imagination was not limited, nor was it abated by such a thing as a *récit.* Mercier refers to the French stage as "notre petite scène de dix pieds quarrés," [14] so pitifully contrasted with the scope of Shakespeare's. Mercier praises the English poet for his respect of history, his plenitude of ideas, his faithfulness to detail. The meaningful rediscovery of this "vaste génie" is summarized in the following quotation: "Enfin, Shakespeare a paru tout entier, et c'était rendre en France un service à l'art dramatique." [15]

---

[13] Mercier did *retouchements* of *King Lear, Romeo and Juliet,* and *Timon of Athens.* See Béclard, p. 323.
[14] Mercier, *Mon bonnet de nuit,* III, 162-163.
[15] *Ibid.,* p. 284.

Just as unshakeable and unbending as his proposition to overthrow cherished dramatic principles is Mercier's other great conviction: his tenacious belief in the moral purpose of drama. As part of his idea that the perfection of dramatic poetry lies ahead, he states first the concept of the useful writer, who has a great privilege in that he instructs mankind. The poet, as a "bienfaiteur," can teach us what is good and honest; in exercising *sensibilité*, "cette force invincible et puissante," he opens the treasures of the human heart and instructs us in the qualities of sincerity and virtue. According to Mercier, two of these virtues, which we can learn, are pity and commiseration; and one cannot be softened too much by these elements (pp. 1-12). He finds, moreover, that "un attendrissement perpétuel serait l'état le plus délicieux pour l'homme." [16] The theater is made to rectify those who have a bad vision of life, to aid the intelligence of the mediocre, to teach men what they should hate, love, and esteem. So it is that the dramatic poet must become the poet of the eighteenth century; his theater must be more extensive, his characters more varied. All this Mercier declares, advocating a type of *drame* where monarchs sleep and mores of the present come to the forefront (pp. 15-16).

Further responsibilities of the dramatist are stated. Public interest must penetrate his soul, and once this has occurred, the playwright will sense exactly what he owes to the assembly of men. The writer must "respirer dès l'enfance dans les bras de la simplicité des mœurs et de la vertu" (p. 217). Having accepted this exalted idea of human nature, and continuing to believe that man is born good, the poet uses his pen as would the king his scepter; it must, therefore, not fall into the mire, but must be lifted continually above error and concealed vice. The dramatist must be inflamed with truth and always enthusiastic for virtue. His creations should show man's grandeur, and his heroes are to be admired, causing the common man to secretly blush when he compares himself to these lofty characters. Corneille seized this purpose, says Mercier, and this is why he has been and will

---

[16] Mercier, *Mon bonnet de nuit*, II, 7.

continue to be admired; this is why he remains the favorite of great souls (pp. 216-220).

Mercier's concern for the patriotic, nationalistic facet of drama stamps him as something of a precursor of Marie-Joseph Chénier [17] and the *tragédie nationale*. Mercier recognizes Corneille as the "restaurateur de la tragédie" in France, but laments the fact that he was not born in Rome or in London, where the force of liberty and republicanism had been felt. Corneille's genius would then have had worthy audiences; it would have influenced the men who took part in the legislation of their government, men who were ready to fight for liberty. Racine, Corneille's successor, is seen by Mercier as a man lacking the "génie politique" of his predecessor. With Racine, tragedy became "un tableau tracé de fantaisie, comme les batailles d'Alexandre ou celles de Constantin" (p. 27). Thus the French, continues Mercier, are still far from a national tragedy; for love has been established as the "moteur principal de leurs pièces: ils avaient à parler à un peuple de

---

[17] Marie-Joseph Chénier (1764-1811) expounded his ideas on the *tragédie nationale* in an *épître dédicatoire* and in the *Discours préliminaire* for his tragedy, *Charles IX* (Paris: Didot jeune, 1790). He states that he wishes to make of the theater "une école de vertu et de liberté." (*Ibid.*, p. 6) His idea of tragedy embraces the majestic, the simple, the evocation of pity and admiration, the inspiration of hate for tyranny and superstition, and the respect for law and morality. Chénier claims that in Athens, only national plays were presented, and that drama in Greece was directly connected to public celebration. (*Ibid.*, p. 10.) He then explains why a real *tragédie nationale* has heretofore been inconceivable in France: the regime of Cardinal Richelieu made this genre an impossibility, as did "la servitude des pensées sous le règne de Louis XIV." Even Voltaire, the enemy of superstition, "a plus approfondi, dans ses tragédies, la morale proprement dite, que la politique;" these same obstacles which prevented Corneille and Racine from representing their nation in the theater, still existed for Voltaire. (*Ibid.*, pp. 11-18) Chénier recognizes that now the propitious moment for his tragedy to be presented has arrived. He will use no *confidents;* only illustrious, historical characters will carry out his action. (*Ibid.*, pp. 18-19) No *galanterie* is to be shown, for tragedy "doit peindre les passions humaines dans leur plus grande énergie." (*Ibid.*, p. 25) There is not a scene in *Charles IX*, says Chénier, which does not inspire "l'horreur du fanatisme, des guerres civiles, du parjure, et de l'adulation cruelle et intéressée. La vertu y est exaltée, le crime puni par le mépris et par le remords, la cause du peuple et des lois défendue sans cesse contre les courtisans et la tyrannie." (*Ibid.*, pp. 26-27) Chenier affirms that his *Charles IX* is the only true *tragédie nationale* which has yet appeared in France. He hopes to serve the cause of a beneficial and courageous philosophy in an enlightened nation. (*Ibid.*, pp. 27-28).

femmes." Tragedy has become, in essence, "un pur roman" (pp. 28-29).

A true, real tragedy, however, will enlighten the people about their true interests and will exalt a brighter patriotism in their hearts. Tragedy, as Mercier envisions it in its nationalistic drapings, will cause the nation to cherish its homeland. Unveiling the abuses of his century, the poet will be able to influence public opinion, using it to strike out against odious laws (pp. 39-41). Tragedy then will raise its proud and august head in free states where it has freed itself of bad qualities. The name of the poet will be united to that of legislator, and the people will be taught what paths lead to despotism. An eventual national tragedy will thus be created (p. 45). At the same time, the dramatic poet, working in this fashion for the good of the state, will assume the imprint of dignity.[18]

Mercier includes in his concept of the strong moral purpose of the drama the theory that tragedy must be answerable to the secret vices of man, showing them in all their villainy (p. 41). Following this plan, one will represent on the stage the voluptuous man, the frivolous man, the prodigal, the debtor, and the atheist (pp. 113-114). Using all his resources to describe what is good, the dramatist is also to show the shame of lie and ingratitude. The corruptor is presented and then punished; the envious man appears, recognizes finally his vice, and believes the contrary of what he had formerly affirmed (pp. 127-131). Mercier does not, however, sanction the presentation of such a thing as "la passion incestueuse de Phèdre." He describes, in the following passage, his inability to accept this in drama:

> Cette déclaration d'amour faite à son beau-fils, doit enflammer les joues de la pudeur, et faire rougir toute personne de son sexe. Ses fureurs, lorsqu'elle apprend l'arrivée de son époux, révoltent le sens moral. Je ne sais à quoi peut servir le tableau de cette passion effrenée, exposée sans ménagement sous le regard de tous les âges.[19]

---

[18] Mercier, *Mon bonnet de nuit*, II, 125.
[19] *Ibid.*, p. 124.

The performance of *Phèdre* should, in fact, be forbidden, because the details of this tragedy give the idea of a dissoluteness that would be more suitable if covered by a veil. The poet, however, does not always have to show innocence and virtue rewarded; for, indeed, he must reveal all the calamities which await us.[20] He should familiarize the spectator with "les touches sombres qui composent le fatal tableau de la condition humaine," and thus the crime does not always have to be punished (pp. 247-251).

The following statement in *Mon Bonnet de nuit* serves almost as a summary of Mercier's credo on the subject of drama:

> Mais la poésie par excellence, est la poésie dramatique; c'est alors qu'elle est noble, utile, majestueuse; sa voix rappelle l'honneur antique, et tire de l'oubli les actions généreuses; elle les immortalise; elle reconduit l'homme dans les routes sacrées de la nature: tantôt elle introduit l'homme superbe dans les tristes foyers de la vertueuse indigence, et lui commande les pleurs... c'est dans la poésie dramatique que l'âme sensible de l'homme est mise à découvert; et interrogée de toute part, la nature y parle sa langue énergique; on y voit toute la force des passions, et ce cours vivant de morale nous apprend à connaître l'homme, et à avoir une idée plus grande de l'espèce humaine.[21]

The dramatic poet, conceived by the mind of Mercier, is a universal painter, capturing every detail of human life. The royal cloak is indifferent to his brush, as is the peasant's coarse garment; it is the heart of man which he is seeking and which he is to examine. "Tout lui est précieux, dès que la chose est vraie et peut ajouter à la fidélité du tableau."[22]

Mercier's theories approach in many ways those of his contemporaries, especially Diderot and Beaumarchais; but Mercier proceeds along a radical pathway with a more vehement attack on the unities, a more pronounced emphasis on the moral purpose

---

[20] In the preface to this *drame, Jenneval*, Mercier also states that in the theater, passion is to be rendered "redoutable autant qu'elle est dangereuse." See *Théâtre complet* (Amsterdam: B. Vlam, 1778), I, 3.

[21] Mercier, *Mon bonnet de nuit*, IV, 175-176.

[22] Mercier, *Théâtre complet*, Preface to *La Brouette du vinaigrier*, III, 116.

of the theater, a greater stress on the national, patriotic side to drama than other critics. He also evidences perhaps a more lasting appreciation of Shakespeare than is observed among other contemporaries.[23] It has been noted that if Mercier's theories relative to tragedy and the *drame* are overstatements of Diderot's dramatic philosophy, then they are exaggerations which advance theory in the direction of Constant, Hugo, and Romanticism. While applying injury to insult, Mercier's theory represents a discarding of the tradition of the *grand siècle*,[24] a casting away of poetics, and a transference of the theater to a realm where the *pathétique* and the sentimental are fused with the moral.

---

[23] Pusey, pp. 7-9.
[24] *Ibid.*, p. 9.

CHAPTER VIII

LA HARPE

Jean-François de la Harpe (1739-1803), in his earlier years a disciple of Voltaire, was already an established journalist, poet, dramatist, and critic when in 1786[1] he began a long series of lectures at the Musée de Monsieur, reorganized in 1785 as a literary society and renamed the "Lycée."[2] Interrupted by the Revolution, La Harpe's efforts were resumed in 1796. His lectures began to be published in 1799 under the title *Lycée ou Cours de littérature*, and in six years comprised sixteen volumes. A study which deals mainly with seventeenth century literature, it is the most complete expression[3] of La Harpe's literary tenets and critical evaluations.[4]

La Harpe immediately recognizes that tragedy in France, as among the Greeks, has occupied a superior position in the rank and order of genres.[5] As an imitation of a serious action, tragedy does not admit a mingling of the serious and the comic, nor the combination "du grave et du burlesque" (I, 56). This mixing of two opposites is a type of barbarism evident in the plays of the

---

[1] René Wellek, *A History of Modern Criticism: 1750-1950* (4 vols.; New Haven: Yale University Press, 1955), I, 66.
[2] Grace Mildred Sproull, *The Critical Doctrine of Jean-François de la Harpe* (Chicago: University of Chicago Libraries, 1939), p. 2.
[3] Other works pertinent to tragedy, the *Eloge de Racine* and the *Essai sur les trois tragiques grecs*, were reproduced in large part in the *Lycée*.
[4] Wellek, I, 66-67.
[5] Jean-François de la Harpe, *Lycée ou Cours de littérature* (16 vols.; Paris: Deterville, 1818), I, 48. Subsequent citations in parentheses refer to this work and this specific edition.

English and the Spanish. Although imitation is a source of pleasure, one must not believe, says La Harpe, that "tout soit également imitable" (I, 43). One must imitate with choice; for, as he remarks in the preface to his *drame, Barnevel,* "Nous n'admettons sur la scène que cette nature choisie qui est l'objet de tous les arts d'imitation." [6] Tragedy is, moreover, essentially heroic, and this characteristic, combined with the dignity of characters, separates it from the *drame* and the *tragédie bourgeoise,* which do not have "l'appareil de la représentation, ni l'intérêt attaché aux grands événements, aux noms célèbres, aux révolutions des Empires, aux moeurs des peuples." [7] The sublime is the soul of tragedy, and the *drame* cannot rise to this. Of the three areas which tragedy can treat, "l'histoire, la fable, et les sujets d'imagination," the last two are more suited to provide a basis for interest:

> ... la Fable, parce que le merveilleux de la religion autorise celui des événements, et amène des situations, et même des caractères hors de l'ordre commun; les sujets d'invention, parce que le poète, maître des événements et des caractères, peut les disposer à son gré pour les effets du théâtre... (IX, 275-276).

Superior to comedy by virtue of its numerous and diverse facets, tragedy presents a challenge which only a great talent is capable of meeting. Tragedy is, moreover,

> ... une mine abondante, mais très pénible à fouiller, et qui ne peut être exploitée qu'à grands frais. Quelle force de tête ne faut-il pas pour soutenir sur la scène un grand caractère donné par l'histoire? Quelle solidité de jugement pour en observer toutes les convenances, pour les adapter à l'effet théâtral, pour bien représenter les moeurs nationales et n'en prendre que ce qu'elles ont de dramatiques (XI, 285-286).

In addition, the great problem of the tragedian is that of uniting what La Harpe calls "la grande force de tête et la grande sensibilité du coeur (XI, 286).

---

[6] Jean-François de la Harpe, *Œuvres* (16 vols., Paris: Pissot, 1778), I, 151.

[7] *Ibid.,* pp. 156-158.

La Harpe embraces the idea of the imperfect tragic hero. The mixture of good and evil, the tragic flaw are elements natural to the human heart, as Phèdre well illustrates. One cannot judge a play by the principles of society, and therefore not all characters must be irreproachable from a moral standpoint (I, 68). Our critic does not agree, however, with Aristotle's recommendation that virtuous men must not be shown passing from good to evil fortune. Britannicus and Hippolyte are examples of worthy characters whose fall excites pity, and in no way revolts us. La Harpe does agree with Aristotle that the evil man experiencing a shift from bad to good fortune is ill-suited for tragedy, just as the punishment of a tyrant or wicked man serves no purpose and excites neither terror nor pity (I, 66-67). In true Aristotelian fashion, La Harpe reminds the reader that a general principle of tragedy is the requirement that each character act and speak according to his known character. A king will not express himself as a commoner, for all elevated personages must speak a language worthy of their rank. Their speech must conform to their character; it must be adapted to their interests, to their passions, to their dangers. The separation which exists between ordinary language and the language of tragedy is essential and indispensable. It should always be maintained. Corneille, as his first service to the theater, presented nobleness of language. It was he who marked the limits between tragic diction and ordinary discourse (V, 169-171).

Like Voltaire, Diderot, Marmontel, and Grimm, La Harpe shows great interest in the theater of the ancients. Establishing as his premise the idea that the French cannot judge their theater and that of the Greeks by the same rules, he proceeds to enumerate certain differences which alienate the two systems of tragedy. He mentions the nature of the Greek tonge which lent naturalness to speeches in the language and which gave facility to versification. La Harpe also finds that tragedy among the Greeks was "toujours renfermée dans leur propre histoire," while French tragedy can seek subjects from all parts of the known world. The French also bear a spirit different from the Greeks who attended their spectacle, not as "une assemblée choisie," but as "un peuple" witnessing a dramatic production given on a state occasion and paid for by the republic (I, 60; 273-76). The immenseness of the Greek theater, their "décorations magnifiques" (on which La Harpe does not elaborate), their masks — all these elements — sought to please the eyes and ears rather than to create an illusion in the mind of the spectator. The more restricted quality of the French theater is elucidated:

> Nous sommes renfermés dans des bornes locales très étroites, et les objets d'illusion, vus de plus près, doivent être ménagés avec une vraisemblance beaucoup plus rigoureuse. Nous parlons à une classe d'hommes choisis, dont le goût, exercé par l'habitude de juger tous les jours, est nécessairement plus sévère, et dont l'âme accoutumée aux émotions, n'en est que plus difficile à émouvoir. Sans aucun objet qui puisse les distraire et flatter leurs sens, ils peuvent s'armer de toute la rigueur de leur raison, et sont encore plus disposés à juger qu'à sentir. Il n'y a là aucune distraction favorable au poète; lui seul est chargé de tout, et on ne lui fait grâce de rien (I, 275).

In the French theater, there is no music to charm the ear, no chorus to replace the action. The dramatic poet must always come to the point, despite the fact that many times there is only one idea to be treated during the five acts; the dramatist must maintain curiosity with sometimes only one event; he is forced, moreover, to calm the restlessness of the spectator, who wishes no respite from the progression of the drama. This contrast represents, therefore, some of the difficulties of the modern playwright working with a genre "où il faut cacher la poésie aussi soigneusement qu'ils [les grecs] la montraient" (I, 276).

In spite of restriction and handicap, the moderns, through the exploration of sentiment and passion, have made advances, and continue to drive ahead into "une situation théâtrale"; contemporary dramatists stir the heart more powerfully, and they know better how to vary and multiply different emotions (I, 276-277). La Harpe furthermore avows that the French have carried "plus loin que les anciens l'art de la contexture dramatique, et mieux connu les ressources nécessaires pour soutenir une intrigue pendant cinq actes" (I, 383). He also finds that if ancient tragedy was "plus sévèrement héroïque," then French tragedy can boast of being "plus touchante" (VI, 84).

Pity and fear as elements of tragedy greatly occupy La Harpe's thoughts. He considers them mainly in relation to Aristotelian catharsis, seeking to establish a valid interpretation of this perplexing facet of the tragic experience. He begins by citing Corneille's concept of the role which pity and fear play. La Harpe recalls that the seventeenth century tragedian felt that the spectator experiences a certain pity and fear by seeing his fellow man fall into misfortune. This reaction in turn leads to the fear of a similar fate for ourselves, a fear which is coupled, nevertheless, with the desire to avoid such mishap and the wish to purge from our being the passion responsible for the misfortune of the people we pity (I, 54). La Harpe finds that the logic here is sound, but that Aristotle's words should be interpreted as follows:

> ... l'objet de toute imitation théâtrale, au moment même où elle excite la pitié et la terreur en nous montrant des actions feintes, est d'adoucir, de modérer en nous ce que cette pitié et cette terreur auraient de trop pénible, si les actions que l'on nous représente étaient réelles (I, 54-55).

Who would be able, asks La Harpe, to bear the misfortunes of Oedipus or Andromaque, if these misfortunes existed under our eyes in actual reality. The tragedy would harm us rather than afford us pleasure (I, 55). Thus the dramatic illusion, working together with the element of catharsis, is responsible for the removal of the bitter and distressing qualities of the tragedy (I, 271).

La Harpe does not find that pity is a dangerous passion: indeed, most moral virtues, those which are most valuable for society, are related to pity. Tragedy of the present

> ... nous attendrit sans danger, porte dans notre âme toutes les émotions qui exercent et augmentent notre sensibilité, nous touche de compassion pour le malheur, nous soulève d'indignation contre le crime, nous transporte d'admiration pour la vertu, et grave en nous de grandes et utiles vérités avec le burin de la poésie. Voilà l'objet de l'art dramatique, art beaucoup plus étendu qu'il n'était du temps d'Aristote (I, 272).

La Harpe recognizes that since the time of Aristotle, the "dénouement malheureux" has been regarded as the most tragic. It has been observed, continues our critic, that the sadness which this type of denouement evokes, is not in itself the most perfect element of dramatic art. With a reference which almost leads us to his previous explanation of catharsis, La Harpe explains that pity and terror should have their sweetness and their charm, and that when we assemble in a theater, "les impressions mêmes qui nous font le plus de mal doivent pourtant nous faire plaisir, parce que, sans cela, il n'y avait aucune différence entre la réalité et l'illusion" (IX, 317). The great merit of the tragedian is that of finding the suitable degree of emotion, the point at which terror and pity become a pleasure (XI, 386).

La Harpe decrees that the marvellous can be used in tragedy, but only under certain conditions: "...ou comme moyen, ou en action." Racine uses it "comme moyen" in *Iphigénie*. Here the oracle which demands the sacrifice of the princess justifies not only Agamemnon's behavior, but serves also as a foundation for the whole play. As for the marvellous "en action," there is more of a difficulty involved. Ancient tragedians, such as Euripides and Sophocles, had no scruples about incorporating it into the action, and both divinities and ghosts appeared on the stage. Later, by decree of Horace, these extraordinary means were not to become a part of the work, except in the case of absolute necessity. Up until the time of Voltaire, continues La Harpe, the marvellous was banished from the French theater and exiled to the realm of the opera. He recalls that Voltaire, in his preface to *Sémiramis*, states that the hesitation over using the marvellous has no justification, and that "appuyé sur les idées religieuses reçues chez toutes les nations," it does not offend *raison* or *bienséance* (X, 91-92).

If it is a question of treating a recent event or depicting the mores of a neighboring country, history, contends La Harpe, must not be strangely disfigured. When, for example, an event which has occurred in England is presented on the Parisian stage, the playwright should not be permitted to contradict the truth of actual fact or belie the mores of that country, at least to the point that an Englishman attending the play could not restrain his laughter. The foreign spectator should think he is in London, and if he believes this to be true, then the duty of the dramatic poet has been fulfilled (VI, 158). Mores are part of theatrical imitation; as such, they are not necessarily good, but at least they are subordinate not only to certain circumstances, but also to the time and the country where the action takes place (V. 187). Racine knew, as La Harpe remarks, that the essential duty of the dramatic poet was to be faithful in his depiction of mores. This is seen in his handling of the Romans in *Britannicus,* the Jews in *Athalie,* the Turks in *Bajazet* (V, 376).

Although La Harpe considers himself a friend of the rules,[8] he immediately minimizes the importance of the unities of time and place, characterizing them succinctly as "deux choses qui ne feront jamais le sort d'un ouvrage" (V, 287). In another section of the *Lycée*, he interprets the unity of time in its Aristotelian sense, declaring that this twenty-four hour rule has a "latitude raisonnable," without which the dramatic poet would be deprived of several interesting subjects. The addition of several hours to the calculation is not to be regarded as a serious infraction of the rule (I, 49). In his own tragedy *Coriolan,* La Harpe extends the unity of place by having the action take place, partly in Rome, and the remainder outside the city walls. In the preface to the tragedy, he justifies this liberty by stating that without it, he could not have treated the subject, and that the basic preservation of the rules is the essential concern: "La proximité des lieux sauve la vraisemblance, qui est le fondement de toute règle; et sans cette extension raisonnable donnée à la loi, il aurait fallu se priver de plus d'un sujet très heureux."[9]

La Harpe confirms his belief in the unity of action by condemning "tous ces épisodes étrangers, ces morceaux de rapport." He further justifies this unity by stating that Aristotle's idea on the subject is "la plus complète et la plus juste qu'on puisse se former de la contexture d'un drame" (I, 61). Plays by Lope de Vega and Shakespeare [10] contain so many events that the best memory would hardly be able to retain them after the performance.

---

[8] Sproull, pp. 16-17.
[9] *Ibid.,* p. 16.
[10] In a miscellaneous essay, *De Shakespeare,* La Harpe praises the French theater and declares that despite the acclaim given this English poet by translators and disciples, such plays as *The Tempest* and *Othello* (which are carefully analyzed) will never replace the greatness of *Athalie* or *Zaïre.* La Harpe also recognizes that Shakespeare has been poorly translated. See: *Oeuvres,* I, 341-484.

These foreign plays, "hors de la mesure convenable," have offended *bon sens*. Good taste, in the eyes of La Harpe, consists of grasping what is the correct *mesure*, that is, "le juste et le nécessaire." As spectators, we are susceptible only to a certain degree of attention, to a certain duration of amusement, instruction, and pleasure (I, 57-58).

La Harpe definitely establishes himself as a proponent of verse and rhyme, and through his statements concerning these elements convinces us, moreover, that the struggle between the poets and the *prosateurs* was by no means a dead issue in the waning years of the eighteenth century. The difficulties of versification, according to him, have taken away none of the truth, none of the precision and accuracy of the tragic poem; in fact, these exigencies have added "un charme inséparable des vers harmonieux" (IX, 165). This idea of difficulty is further explained:

> La difficulté à vaincre, non seulement ajoute aux beaux-arts un charme de plus grand quand elle est vaincue, mais elle ouvre une source abondante de nouvelles beautés. Il ne faut pas prostituer les honneurs d'un aussi bel art que la poésie (I, 50).

If one could be a poet in prose, too many people would then wish to be so; and there are far too many of these already. The superiority of fine verse to the best prose can be explained in terms of the embellishment of detail; and in the case of Corneille's *Cinna:*

> ... la mesure et l'harmonie ont gravé dans tous les esprits et mis dans toutes les bouches ce qui demeurait comme enseveli dans les écrits d'un philosophe, et n'existait que pour un petit nombre de lecteurs. Cette précision, commandée par le rhythme poétique, a tellement consacré les paroles que Corneille prête à Auguste, qu'on croirait qu'il n'a pu s'exprimer autrement; et la conversation d'Auguste et de Cinna ne sera jamais autre chose que les vers qu'on a retenus de Corneille (V, 220).

La Harpe also asserts that rhyme is essential to versification, at least in modern languages. It is "voisine de la monotonie," but in itself is agreeable, just as is every type of symmetrical recurrence. La Harpe reminds his reader of the strange *novateurs*, like La Motte, who wished to abandon rhyme, but who knew less about what they discussed than did Voltaire, who deemed both verse and rhyme necessary (V, 53). After warning against *enjambement*, La Harpe suggests variation in the alexandrine:

> Le moyen qu'ont employé nos bons poètes, c'est de placer de temps en temps des césures ou des repos à différentes places, en sorte qu'un vers ne ressemble pas à l'autre; de ne pas toujours procéder par distiques, et de finir quelquefois le sens en faisant attendre la rime (V, 77).

In considering love as a tragic passion, La Harpe pronounces "l'amour malheureux" as the most abundant source of the *pathétique*. As he states in several places in the *Lycée* (I, 276; 327; V, 284), the ancients did not utilize this passion in their tragedies. This is true, he says, if one excludes the role of Phaedra. It remained for the moderns to learn that love, "comme ressort tragique, suffirait pour rendre l'art beaucoup plus riche et plus étendu ... qu'il ne pouvait l'être chez eux" (I, 69). Love is a passion, however, which should command. When Corneille created his tragedies, it was the vogue to depict love as one would see it in a *roman;* in his works it became "l'exagération la plus romanesque" (V, 283-284). With Racine a new art came into being which demonstrated love as "cette passion forcenée traînant après elle le crime et le remords" (V, 285). In Pyrrhus, Oreste, and Hermione, love is indeed tragic; these characters exhibit Racine's wise and expressive presentation of this passion which is based not on astonishment, admiration, and idealistic nature, but on "une nature toujours vraie," and a knowledge of the human heart (V, 324; 334). If Racine is the first tragedian to treat love in a superior fashion — and in the eyes of La Harpe he well deserves this credit — then Voltaire must be praised for setting Racine free from the prejudice which credited the author of *Phèdre* with the debilitation of tragedy through his great preoccupation with love. It was also Voltaire who showed that Corneille had made tragedy insipid by the use of *galanterie* (VI, 86).

According to La Harpe, love combatted and resisted by outside forces and obstacles is never as interesting as when it is attacked by the torments which spring from the passion itself: "... les plus grands maux d'amour n'étaient pas ordinairement ceux qui lui viennent d'ailleurs, mais ceux qu'il se fait à lui-même" (V, 340). La Harpe does, however, issue a warning to Frenchmen who might possibly allow their preference for "les sujets d'amour" to limit their pleasure or misguide their judgement:

> Trop de gens sont portés à regarder comme des ouvrages froids ceux où l'amour ne joue pas un très grand rôle, et nous en avons de très beaux qui n'ont point cette sorte d'intérêt. Mais quoi donc! n'y en aurait-il plus d'autre? L'amour est-il le seul sentiment dramatique? La tragédie n'a-t-elle pas une foule d'autres ressorts qu'elle met en œuvre tout aussi heureusement, et souvent avec plus de mérite? (I, 328)

An author does not exhibit coldness in his work simply because he has not employed love as its principal element. The fifth act of *Cinna*, the fourth act of *Horace*, for example, make us weep; they also elevate us, and at the same time produce *attendrissement*. La Harpe suggests that each type of tragedy be put in its proper place, and that above all, a preference never become an exclusion (I, 328-329).

La Harpe, assuredly one of the last of the neo-classicists, is, however, given to certain liberal tendencies. In the presence of a man such as Mercier, La Harpe defends the unities,[11] but the view of them which we grasp in the *Lycée* is a flexible one. He accuses his contemporaries of abusing the word *sensibilité*, and at the same time it becomes a frequently-used word in his criticism; this tendency reflects perhaps some pre-Romantic trends on the part of La Harpe.[12] His attachment to Aristotle, Horace, and Boileau is undeniable, and for the most part, his credo is an offspring of seventeenth-century doctrine. La Harpe regards the rules as aids, however, not as absolute standards. It is the power of rational thought which may show the writer when he can depart from certain precepts. La Harpe emerges, therefore, as a

---

[11] La Harpe, *Œuvres*, I, *op. cit.*, pp. 446-448.
[12] Sproull, pp. 25-26.

typical eighteenth-century modifier of seventeenth century principles, a follower of the example of neo-classicism which Voltaire had instituted.[13]

---

[13] Sproull, *op. cit.*, p. 27.

CHAPTER IX

CONCLUSION

With *Athalie*, the great century of French tragedy ends; and in the period of decline which followed, the critics sense almost helplessly the impoverishment of the genre. With eyes cast in the direction of true excellence, they maintain an elevated concept of tragedy. Even Fénelon, writing within the shadow of the great Racine, criticizes his contemporaries for the romanesque elements which they have allowed to invade tragedy. He sees the genre as a marvellously strong, natural creation endowed with the heritage of the ancients, and presenting great events and violent passions. The Abbé Du Bos, likewise, considers it as a form which must depict the impetuous, a work to be filled with dignity, and soaring far above the ordinary in character and declamation. Houdar de la Motte, classic in form, although innovational in spirit, decrees that tragedy must be an important action. As one of the outstanding literary genres, it must imitate "une nature choisie" and herein lies his link with La Harpe, who wrote of this same *nature* [1] over a half-century later. The Abbé Batteux recognizes in tragedy the heroic, the conflict of great interests, the depiction of extraordinary feats, the revelation of strength seen in characters who are superior to other men. The journalistic critics recall for their readers the past glory of French tragedy, and tell of the glorious heights to

---

[1] Antoine de Rivarol (1753-1801), who achieved some distinction as a critic on the basis of his *discours*, *De l'universalité de la langue française* (1784), speaks therein of this same idea of a *nature choisie*. Art, says Rivarol, is never as great or as large as is nature; the former must always make a choice. See: *Oeuvres complètes* (5 vols.; Paris: Collin, 1808), II, 85.

which it climbed in the preceding century. Grimm, particularly, while lamenting the present state of French tragedy, calls for an imitation of the majestic naiveté of the ancients, for their sublimity and simplicity. He is a severe interpreter of the drama of his age; his standards are high, and for the most part they are geared to the high ideals of the seventeenth-century theater. Marmontel's theory reveals a lofty idea of tragedy. The language is to be elevated above the commonplace; it is to be more sustained and more noble than in actual society, and is to be pronounced by characters of high rank. Du Bos, La Harpe, and Fénelon realize that tragedy possesses a superiority over comedy, and this conviction is explained by the importance of tragedy's subject, the elevation of its style, the necessity for its simplicity and nobility. La Harpe, on the threshold of a new era, still regards tragedy as a challenge which only great talent is capable of meeting. As a superior genre, as an imitation of a serious action, tragedy admits no mingling of the serious and the comic; but the problem of the tragedian, however, is that of uniting "la grande force de tête et la grande sensibilité du coeur."

After the production of the *Cid*, love came to play so great a role in tragic composition, that now, in the eighteenth century, the critics are prepared to evaluate its validity. Recognizing *galanterie* as love's weakest manifestation, they are ready to censure this romanesque element. Fénelon sadly admits that the "intrigue galante" has become an essential part of tragedy. He would prefer to see "cet amour volage et déréglé," a passion represented as violent. Voltaire and his disciple La Harpe find that love in tragedy is often only *galanterie*,[2] and that to be worthy of the tragic theater, this passion must form a natural part of the action; it must be shown in all its danger, leading the hero to misfortune and crime. Love, if it is to appear in tragedy, must be, moreover, the dominating tyrant, barbarous and deadly. Both in theory and practice, Voltaire maintains that superior tragedy can be written without treating love; and as proof, he cites *Athalie* and *Mérope*

---

[2] Elie-Catherin Fréron (1719-1776), known today chiefly as the enemy of Voltaire and the editor of the *Année Littéraire*, a journal which first appeared in 1754, also expressed the view that love, not *galanterie*, should dominate the action of tragedy. See: Robert L. Myers, "Fréron's Theories on Tragedy," *The French Review*, XXXI (May, 1958), 503-504.

as examples. La Harpe, at the close of the century, will also evoke the memory of Racine's masterpiece to affirm what Voltaire had said almost four decades previously. Grimm also regards *Athalie* very highly, stating that all men of taste look on this tragedy as the masterpiece of the French stage, and that not destined for the public stage, it is a play which does not use love as its dramatic mainspring. Grimm does, however, reproach Racine for having given French audiences their great taste for this childish passion of love. Contrary to Grimm, Marmontel holds that love is the most theatrical of the passions, the most interesting. He does not, like Fénelon and Grimm, censure French dramatists for their use of love, but chooses to recognize that by using it as an element in drama, they have drawn from an inexhaustible source of poetry. Mercier's strong moral purpose for the theater leads him from the subject of love to a consideration of the more didactic, nationalistic aspects of drama. In Rousseau-like fashion, he banishes the incestuous passion of Phèdre from the stage and turns to a full preoccupation with the rectification of man's evil. Throughout the century, therefore, love is, among the critics, the most discussed of the passions; and in their eyes it is certainly the most interesting and the most abused.

With the exception of Mercier, who views the unities collectively as "la misérable règle," there is no violent attack against this classical ideal. La Motte's introduction of a fourth unity, that of interest, seems to be a desire for *nouveauté*; in fact, in its broadest sense, it might be taken only as an interpretation of the unity of action. At the same time, however, La Motte makes clear that he does not wish to abolish the unities of time and place; although, like Fréron,[3] he is open to experimentation, and feels that there must be a removal of restraint from the playwright with regard to this rule. Voltaire is a staunch defender of the unities. Dismissing the unity of interest, he clings wholeheartedly to tradition, to the heritage of the great masters; the unities must be accepted as wise and essential. Batteux interprets the unity of time in an Aristotelian sense, ascribing to the action a period of twenty-four hours. He will grant no indulgence to the unity of place, although he

---

[3] Myers, *op. cit.,* p. 506.

is aware that it is a rule which creates considerable difficulty for the dramatist. Diderot finds, strangely enough, that the unities are "sensées," and he defends in particular the unity of action and the unity of place. Marmontel endorses an extension of the unity of time, to be justified by the *entr'acte* and the "durée fictive" of the tragedy. This is a liberty, however, which should be bridled by the judgement of the author and not carried to excess in the fashion of the English and the Spanish. La Harpe, although notably conservative, tends to minimize the importance of the unities of time and place. This latter unity he extends both in theory and practice, with the added reminder that it is to be a reasonable extension. He embraces the unity of action in its full Aristotelian sense and condemns, as does Rivarol,[4] the Shakespearean play for its multiplicity of events. We see, therefore, that on the question of the unities, there is no uniformity of thought; but the spirit of this particular classical concept remains intact until the advent of the Romantics.

The merits of prose as opposed to verse and rhyme occupy to a great extent the minds of the eighteenth-century critics. We have seen that early in the century, Fénelon and Du Bos establish themselves as enemies to rhyme. The former labels rhyme as "gênante;" it is a definite hindrance to naturalness in speech. Du Bos describes it as a troublesome chain about the neck of the poet, reducing his work to nothing more than a mechanical process. Harmony and rhythm are more essential than the uniform cadence of the alexandrine. La Motte, in attempting to show the advantages of the prose tragedy, speaks of the tyranny of rhyme and "le hasard des rimes." The bad poet in particular has become a slave to these factors. Despite the need for reform, the alexandrine is in possession of tragedy; but La Motte still maintains that, to establish *vraisemblance*, the poet must have men speak as men, producing thereby a *sentiment* which is truer and more realistic. Voltaire, as in the case of the unities, is a most thorough neo-classicist. It is he who must answer the objections of La Motte, defending as early as 1730 the verse tragedy.[5] Voltaire finds that the alexandrine

---

[4] Rivarol, *Oeuvres complètes*, II, 84-85.
[5] Charles Collé (1709-1783), journalist, critic, and playwright, included in the midst of the reviews, anecdotes, epigrams, and *chansons* of his *Journal*

is full of strength and harmony, that rhyme is a process natural to man, that versification is far from a mechanical task. The question of prose and verse is certainly a major problem considered by Grimm, and to a large extent, his opinion on the matter alienates him from the neo-classical spirit. Like La Motte, he advocates the use of *vers libres* as a substitute for the alexandrine; he does praise Voltaire for his use of *vers croisés* which he finds to be as close to natural discourse as any poetic form yet observed. Grimm's animosity with regard to the alexandrine seems to grow with the years, and by 1770, he has blatantly advocated a prose tragedy. Marmontel and La Harpe maintain the attitude of Voltaire towards verse. The former sees the advantage in its cadence, and this is especially true in relation to the memorization of the actor. Marmontel also states that the artifice of poetry is one of the accessories which tempers the dramatic illusion by removing some of its painful aspects while maintaining at the same time a sufficient amount of naturalness in thought and feeling. La Harpe, like Voltaire, mentions the "difficulté à vaincre" as an added charm for verse in the creation of tragedy. He finds that verse opens an abundant source of new beauties and is superior to prose through its embellishment of detail. Rhyme is essential to versification, despite its monotony and despite the attacks of certain critics such as La Motte, whom he mentions by name. Condillac realizes that the poet must write with more art than the *prosateur*, but with no less naturalness. Poetry is deemed necessary in the writing of tragedy, and composed even in a mediocre fashion, it will please more than the best written prose.[6] Thus there is no uniformity of opinion in the matter — only an undercurrent of resentment against a poetic drama, springing from the attacks of La Motte early in the century, and renewed by Mercier, Grimm, and Diderot in the decade of the seventies. The neo-classicists are still present, however, and at the end of the century, the battle continues to rage.

---

certain dramatic theory. On the subject of the verse tragedy, he denounces prose as unsuitable for the sublime style which tragedy requires. *Journal et mémoires*, ed. Honoré Bonhomme (3 vols.; Paris: Firmin Didot, 1868), II, 183.

[6] *Œuvres* (23 vols.; Paris: C. Houel, 1798), VII, 380-382.

CONCLUSION 115

The critical examination of the theater of the ancients reveals an almost consistent admiration for their simplicity and naturalness. Fénelon speaks of the classical restraint of Sophocles; he praises the modesty, naturalness, and simplicity which characterized certain ancient authors. In his opinion, the hero of French tragedy should emulate, therefore, the loftiness of the classical dramatists; he should speak an unobtrusive dialogue, devoid of all pomposity which is so foreign to the idea of naturalness. Voltaire's *dissertation* preceding *Sémiramis* contains a statement of his admiration for certain Greek dramatic elements. He finds that although these playwrights of antiquity did not perhaps equal the French in *invention*, and although they did not display the shock of passions to be found for example in Racine, they did excel in dignity of presentation. He also recognizes the simplicity of their drama which exhibits one of the characteristics of genius. Grimm praises Sophocles for this same quality of simplicity and for his majestic naiveté. He and Euripides are described as sublime; they are tragedians who possessed "ce grand goût," a quality which the French have yet to acquire. The simplicity of the Greeks will always stand, he says, as a model for everything which represents beauty. Diderot mentions the pomposity of Greek versification and the bombast of their declamation, but adds that these characteristics were well suited not only to their language, but to the spaciousness of their theaters. If the French have conserved the grandiose quality of the ancient theater, they have, on the other hand, abandoned the simplicity of plot, the "conduite simple," and the truth of *tableaux* which existed for the Greeks. Marmontel also acknowledges the simplicity of the ancient theater; he speaks, furthermore, of the Greek dramatic system which was more easily manipulated, since there had to be no explanation for the decrees of destiny. He sees, moreover, that the nuance and delicacy of the moderns would be lost in the vastness of the Greek theater; and that the contrast of passions, which serves as the basis for the modern theater, furnishes movement and situation unknown to ancient dramatists. Mercier, scornful and defiant of France's theatrical heritage, recalls to his readers the naturalness of the Greeks and concludes that his compatriots have ignored the finest characteristics of the ancients. La Harpe, while confirming the simple, natural elements of Greek drama, is inclined to see the limitations imposed by the narrow limits of the French stage, and thereby to account for existing differences in the two systems of drama. La Harpe also finds that the Greeks sought to concentrate on externals, rather than to create an illusion in the minds of the spectators, an illusion which must be handled with more *vraisemblance* and submitted to the approval of a more rigorous taste.

One of the most important manifestations of interest in Aristotle and his *Poetics* is seen in the various interpretations and remarks made by the critics we have studied concerning pity, fear, and the element we speak of as catharsis. Du Bos finds that poets, as well as painters, excite in us an artificial pity and fear by presenting only a copy of an object, which, if real, would be capable of arousing true passion. The impression made by the imitation is, therefore, not as lasting or as serious as the impression which the object itself would have created; and thus its horrible effect is soon erased from our mind. Batteux finds that pity is produced when one views his fellow man in combat with passions and misfortunes; we also fear for the tragic character, but in the state of the unfortunate person in the play. Batteux furthermore interprets catharsis as a purification of pity and fear, a purging of their worst elements, whereby they are made profitable and useful for humanity, and make it possible for us to bear our burdens more easily. La Harpe, like Batteux, sees that the object of the dramatic imitation is to purge from our beings the bad, distressing qualities of pity and fear. We are able to bear the misfortunes of Oedipus, for example, since we realize that the play in reality is a dramatic illusion; accepted as such, the tragedy removes the bitter and discomforting qualities of the tragic experience. Grimm definitely connects the elements of pity and fear to the moral purpose of the theater. While in the theater, the spectator can receive a salutary effect through a frequent shedding of tears. This outpouring of emotion will in turn cause him to be a more sensitive being, while at the same time enlightening him and forming his taste. In the *Commentaire sur Corneille,* Voltaire admits that he does not understand this idea of purgation. He only knows that a sensitive man will experience a noble and delicate pleasure when agitated by the feeling of pity or fear. In the *Dictionnaire philosophique* (Article "Aristotle"), he speaks of Aristotelian catharsis as something of a moral lesson; if the application of this element signifies, for illustration, that one can subdue an incestuous love by observing Phèdre's example, then Voltaire sees no difficulty in reaching an interpretation of this passage in the *Poetics*. Mercier finds that it is necessary to purge only vicious passions, and this can be done through the influencing powers of pity and compassion, through the perfection of a moral sensitivity which induces the spectator to shed tears on behalf of the person enduring misfortune.

One of the great convictions of the eighteenth-century critics is the feeling that the theater of France, and more specifically the tragic genre, stands in need of the revitalizing forces of action and spectacle. Early in the century, La Motte, in a *discours* accompanying *Romulus* (1722), makes a plea for the use of pomp and spectacle. He recognizes that French tragedy is composed largely of *discours* and *récits*, and that with the exception of certain actions not intended for the eyes of a theater audience, there should be more movement and action on the stage instead of "derrière le théâtre." La Motte agrees with Horace on the point that our eyes are more readily impressed than our ears; therefore, the very presence of actors will impress one more than the most carefully written dialogue and *récit*. Early in his career of tragedian, Voltaire added a chorus to his *Œdipe,* and the reintroduction of this Greek element, as he explains it, was in the interest of pomp and display. Later, in the 1731 preface to *Brutus,* he calls for more action while at the same time defining the physical handicaps of the French stage and the limitations which should be imposed by *bienséance*. In 1749, Voltaire is again demanding that tragedy be enhanced by more spectacle, but his desire in this respect is to be regulated by a certain taste which would retain the basic simplicity of the Greek theater. He sees that tragedy is something other than a long conversation, and that by means of natural and beautiful poetry, which is linked to spectacle and pomp,[7] the artistic can be achieved. Marmontel, who also attacks epic traits in tragedy, avows that the resources of *décor* and spectacle open to the French playwright have been

---

[7] Collé attacks the epic qualities of tragedy, which he claims have been popularized by Voltaire. *Journal et mémoires,* I, 73; II, 104; III, 147.

very slight, and that this fact perhaps accounts for the preponderance of *discours* over action. The spoken word, however, can at least offer to the ears that which is denied the eyes. Like Voltaire, Diderot, and Mercier, he attacks poor costuming in the French theater and cites this as another deficiency of the French dramatic system. Grimm adds his voice to those who cry out against the many *discours* which fill French tragedy; he, too, favors action over *récit*. Although Diderot is not interested in great spectacle, he conceives that the graphic, tableau-like effect of drama is a necessity. He, also, envisions the possibility of realistic stage settings and more natural dialogue.

The greatest attack against French tragedy is waged by Mercier, who labels it a ghostlike unreality, pompous, imaginary, and unnatural. His summary rejection of the genre and of the poetics related to it is indeed singular; for despite the recognition that new liberties can be exercised in the field of tragedy, that new elements of revitalization can be utilized, the eighteenth-century critics in general are far from dismissing the rules and theory of days past. They are, however, prepared to study carefully the problems of the tragedian through the eyes of their century.

BIBLIOGRAPHY

BARRAS, MOSES. *The Stage Controversy in France from Corneille to Rousseau.* New York: Institute of French Studies, 1933.

BATTEUX, CHARLES. *Les Beaux-Arts réduits à un même principe.* Paris: Durand, 1747.

———. *Principes de la littérature.* 3 vols. Paris: Desaint et Saillant, 1775.

BÉCLARD, LÉON. *Sébastien Mercier. Sa vie, son œuvre, son temps.* Paris: H. Champion, 1903.

BELEVAL, YVON. *L'Esthétique sans paradoxe de Diderot.* Paris: Gallimard, 1950.

BILLY, A. *Diderot.* Paris: Éditions de France, 1932.

BORGERHOFF, E. B. O. *The Evolution of Liberal Theory and Practice in the French Theater (1680-1757).* Princeton: Princeton University Press, 1936.

BRAUNSCHVIG, MARCEL. *L'Abbé Du Bos. Rénovateur de la critique au XVIIIe siècle.* Toulouse: A. et N. Brun, 1904.

CAZES, ANDRÉ. *Grimm et les Encyclopédistes.* Paris: Les Presses Universitaires, 1933.

CHÉNIER, MARIE-JOSEPH. *Charles IX ou l'École des rois.* Paris: Didot Jeune, 1790.

CHEREL, ALBERT. *Fénelon au XVIIIe siècle.* Paris: Hachette, 1917.

COLLÉ, CHARLES. *Journal et mémoires,* ed. Honoré Bonhomme. 3 vols. Paris: F. Didot, 1868.

———. *Journal historique (1761-1762),* ed. Bever et Boissy. Paris: Mercure de France, 1911.

CONDILLAC, ETIENNE BONNOT DE. *Œuvres.* 23 vols. Paris: C. Houel, 1798.

DESFONTAINES, PIERRE-FRANÇOIS GUYOT, ABBÉ. *Le Nouvelliste du Parnasse.* Paris: Chez Chaubert, 1734.

DIDEROT, DENIS. *Œuvres complètes,* ed. Assézat and Tourneux. 20 vols. Paris: Garnier, 1875-1877.

DU BOS, JEAN-BAPTISTE. *Réflexions critiques sur la poésie et sur la peinture.* 3 vols. Dresde: George Conrad Walther, 1760.

DUPONT, PAUL. *Houdar de la Motte.* Paris: Hachette, 1898.

FELLOWS, OTIS E. and TORREY, NORMAN L. *The Age of Enlightenment.* New York: Appleton-Century-Crofts, 1942.

FÉNELON, FRANÇOIS DE SALIGNAC DE LA MOTHE. *Oeuvres.* 23 vols. Versailles: J. A. Lebel, 1820-30.

FOLKIERSKI, WLADYSLAW. *Entre le classicisme et le romantisme.* Paris: H. Champion, 1925.

GAIFFE, FÉLIX. *Le Drame en France au XVIIIe siècle.* Paris: Collin, 1910.
GRAVIT, FRANCES W. "Notes on the Contents of Fréron's Periodicals," *The Romanic Review,* XXXIV (April, 1943), 116-126.
GRIMM, FRÉDÉRIC MELCHIOR, ET. AL. *Correspondance littéraire,* ed. Maurice Tourneux. 16 vols. Paris: Garnier, 1877-82.
HAINES, C. M. *Shakespeare in France: Criticism to Victor Hugo.* London: Oxford University Press, 1925.
JOANNIDES, A. *La Comédie-Française de 1680 à 1900.* Paris: Plon, 1901.
JONES, ANNE CUTTING. *Frederick Melchior Grimm As a Critic of Eighteenth-Century Drama.* Bryn Mawr: Bryn Mawr College, 1926.
JUSSERAND, J. J. *Shakespeare in France under the Ancien Regime.* London: T. Fisher Unwin, 1899.
LA HARPE, JEAN-FRANÇOIS DE. *Lycée ou Cours de littérature.* 16 vols. Paris: Deterville, 1818.
―――――. *Œuvres.* 6 vols. Paris: Pissot, 1778.
LA MOTTE, ANTOINE HOUDAR DE. *Œuvres.* 10 vols. Paris: Prault, 1753-54.
LANCASTER, HENRY CARRINGTON. *French Tragedy in the Time of Louis XV and Voltaire.* 2 vols. Baltimore: The Johns Hopkins Press, 1950.
LE BRETON, ANDRÉ. *Rivarol, sa vie, ses idées, son talent.* Paris: Hachette, 1895.
LENEL, S. *Un Homme de lettres au XVIIIe siècle. Marmontel.* Paris: Hachette, 1902.
LION, HENRI. *Les Tragédies et les théories dramatiques de Voltaire.* Paris: Hachette, 1895.
LOMBARD, ALFRED. *L'Abbé Du Bos.* Paris: Hachette, 1913.
―――――. *Fénelon et le retour à l'antique au XVIIIe siècle.* Neuchâtel: Secrétariat de l'Université, 1954.
―――――. *La Querelle des anciens et des modernes.* Neuchâtel: Attinger Frères, 1908.
MARMONTEL, JEAN FRANÇOIS. *Œuvres complètes.* 18 vols. Paris: Verdière, 1819.
MERCIER, LOUIS-SÉBASTIEN. *Du théâtre ou Nouvel essai sur l'art dramatique.* Amsterdam: E. Van Harrevelt, 1773.
―――――. *Mon bonnet de nuit.* 4 vols. Neuchâtel: De L'Imprimerie de la Société Typographique, 1784.
―――――. *Tableau de Paris.* 12 vols. Amsterdam, 1783-88.
―――――. *Théâtre complet.* 3 vols. Amsterdam: B. Vlam, 1778.
MORNET, DANIEL. *L'Alexandrin français dans la deuxième moitié du XVIIIe siècle.* Toulouse: Edouard Privat, 1907.
MYERS, ROBERT L. "Fréron's Theories on Tragedy," *The French Review,* XXXI (May, 1958), 503-508.
NAVES, RAYMOND. *Le Goût de Voltaire.* Paris: Garnier, 1938.
NICKLAUS, R. "La portée des théories dramatiques de Diderot et de ses réalisations théâtrales," *The Romanic Review,* LIV (February, 1963), 6-19.
PUSEY, W. W. *Louis-Sébastien Mercier in Germany.* New York: Columbia University Press, 1939.
RIVAROL, ANTOINE. *Œuvres complètes.* 5 vols. Paris: Collin, 1808.
SAINTSBURY, GEORGE E. B. *A History of Criticism.* 3 vols. New York: Dodd, Mead and Company, 1902.
SPROULL, GRACE MILDRED. *The Critical Doctrine of Jean-François de la Harpe.* Chicago: The University of Chicago Libraries, 1939.

VIAL, FRANCISQUE ET DENISE, LOUIS. *Idées et doctrines littéraires du XVIIIe siècle*. Paris: Delagrave, 1930.
VOLTAIRE, FRANÇOIS-MARIE AROUET DE. *Œuvres complètes*, ed. Louis Moland. 52 vols. Paris: Garnier, 1877-85.
WELLEK, RENÉ. *A History of Modern Criticism: 1750-1950*. 4 vols. New Haven: Yale University Press, 1955.
WILSON, ARTHUR M. *Diderot: The Testing Years*. New York: Oxford University Press, 1957.

www.ingramcontent.com/pod-product-compliance
Lightning Source LLC
Chambersburg PA
CBHW020420230426
43663CB00007BA/1254